# Essential
# Scotland

### by Hugh Taylor
### & Moira McCrossan

Above: *the Trossachs. Wilderness of the outlaw Rob Roy MacGregor*

## PASSPORT BOOKS
*NTC/Contemporary Publishing Group*

Above: *Scotch whisky –
the Water of Life in
miniature*

Front cover: *leading a
procession at
Bellahouston Park's
Highland Games in
Glasgow; Loch Katrine in
the Trossachs; blue and
yellow lobster pots*

Back cover: *haggis on
display*

This edition first published in 2000 by Passport Books, a
division of NTC/ Contemporary Publishing Group, Inc.,
4255 West Touhy Avenue, Lincolnwood (Chicago), Illinois
60712–1975 U.S.A.

Published by Passport Books in conjunction with
The Automobile Association of Great Britain.

**Written by Hugh Taylor & Moira McCrossan**

Library of Congress Catalog Card Number: 99-76824
ISBN 0-658-00376-3

Colour separation: Chroma Graphics (Overseas) Pte Ltd,
Singapore

Printed and bound in Italy by Printer Trento srl

# Contents

# About this Book

**Essential *Scotland*** is divided into five sections to cover the most important aspects of your visit to Scotland.

### Viewing Scotland pages 5–14
An introduction to Scotland by the authors.
Scotland's Features
Essence of Scotland
The Shaping of Scotland
Peace and Quiet
Scotland's Famous

### Top Ten pages 15–26
The authors' choice of the Top Ten places to see in Scotland, listed in alphabetical order, each with practical information.

### What to See pages 27–90
The four main areas of Scotland, each with its own brief introduction and an alphabetical listing of the main attractions.
Practical information
Snippets of 'Did you know…' information
3 suggested walks
4 suggested tours
2 features

### Where To... pages 91–116
Detailed listings of the best places to eat, stay, shop, take the children and be entertained.

### Practical Matters pages 117–24
A highly visual section containing essential travel information.

### Maps
All map references are to the individual maps found in the What to See section of this guide.
For example, Edinburgh Castle has the reference ➕ 34C2 – indicating the page on which the map is located and the grid square in which the castle is to be found. A list of the maps that have been used in this travel guide can be found in the index.

### Prices
Where appropriate, an indication of the cost of an establishment is given by **£** signs:
**£££** denotes higher prices, **££** denotes average prices, while **£** denotes lower charges.

### Star Ratings
Most of the places described in this book have been given a separate rating:

✪✪✪    Do not miss
✪✪      Highly recommended
✪       Worth seeing

# Viewing
# Scotland

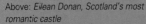

Above: *Eilean Donan, Scotland's most romantic castle*
Right: *Kirkcudbright's ancient market place was marked by this 17th-century Celtic cross*

# The Authors' Scotland

**Celtic Music**

Celtic music is flavour of the moment and comprises the music of the seven Celtic Countries – Scotland, Ireland, Wales, the Isle of Man, Cornwall, Brittany and Galicia – all bound by a common thread but each unique and individual. Essentially a living tradition, it is currently undergoing a renaissance with young musicians experimenting and blending it with jazz and rock. To sample it at its best, head to one of the many pub sessions.

Above: *few sights and sounds can compare with a marching pipe band at Highland Games*
Below: *Goat Fell on the isle of Arran provides the ideal line for a shot to the green*

Some visitors to Scotland are looking for their roots and the ancestors who left these shores centuries earlier. Others come for the scenery, food, golf and culture. To each, however, Scotland is different, and that about sums it up, for trying to describe Scotland is a bit like trying to describe the wind. Just when you think you've got it, it changes direction.

The central belt, industrialised and scarred yet displaying an awesome beauty, includes the two great cities of Edinburgh and Glasgow, contrasting and yet complementing each other. The rolling hills and lush pastures of the South evoke emotions of a time long past, while in the Highlands there's a sense of wilderness created by the towering mountain ranges, dark, mysterious lochs and long, lonely glens.

Scotland is also a land of history where the past is very close. Castles, fortified towers and battlefields from warfaring ages sit beside prehistoric stone monuments the equal of any in Europe.

Then there are the people – independent, argumentative, philosophical – descended from the Celts, integrating successive waves of Italian, Asian and Polish immigrants along the way. We are the Scots and we take great delight in introducing visitors to our food, culture, history, music, sport and politics. Talk to us, join us in song and dance while we celebrate everything and anything in the pubs, bars and at ceilidhs (➤ 38). But take care, you might never want to go home.

# Scotland's Features

## Geography

The popular image of Scotland is of heather-clad mountains, rivers, islands and lochs. The total land area is 77,080sq km (30,405 square miles), much of it sparsely populated islands and mountainous areas. Scotland has around 800 islands, of which about 130 are inhabited. Because of the number of islands and the numerous long sea lochs and estuaries, the 10,000-km (6,215-mile) coastline is vast in relation to the size of the country. The Cairngorms in the north of Scotland is the largest area of peaks over 1,000m in the UK and includes the highest mountain, Ben Nevis, at 1,344m. There are about 30,000 lochs and 50,000km (30,000 miles) of river, which are among the least polluted in the world.

## Climate

The north of Shetland, on the same latitude as the south of Greenland, is closer to the Arctic circle than to London, however, the climate of Scotland in general is temperate but changeable. The Gulf Stream, which bathes the west coast in a warm flow of water from the Gulf of Mexico, moderates temperatures in the west, while rain blows in from the Atlantic. The east tends to be cooler and drier. In the Highlands, snow is common in winter, often closing roads completely.

## Population

The population of Scotland is 5,136,000, most of which is concentrated in the central belt, the broad lowland area between Glasgow and Edinburgh. Scotland is one of the least densely populated areas of Europe – around 66 persons per sq km.

*Spectacular view over the snow-scattered Cairngorms from Cairngorm summit*

**Politics and Society**
Scotland is divided into 32 local authorities ranging in size from tiny Clackmannanshire to the City of Glasgow. In 1999, Scotland elected the first Scottish parliament for 300 years, taking over responsibility for all domestic matters from education and health to roads and transportation. Areas such as foreign policy and social security remain within the jurisdiction of the UK parliament.

# Essence of Scotland

## Horridge
Horridge – a combination of horrid and porridge – is a collection of poems by the Dumfriesshire poet Hugh McMillan, taking a satirical swipe at Scottish kitsch from tartan to shortbread tins and tea towels.
*'Here's tae us*
*Wha's like us*
*Damn few*
*And they're a' on teatowels.'*

*Queen Victoria's favourite view of Loch Tummel*

When Bonnie Prince Charlie fled from Culloden in 1746, he left behind the recipe for Drambuie, a famous whisky-based liqueur, and a legend that launched a thousand biscuit tins. The legislation banning kilt and tartan was ultimately repealed and they were popularised by Walter Scott, and later by Queen Victoria's love affair with the Highlands. The kitsch and sentimental nonsense spawned from these times bore little resemblance to the real Scotland, but with the passage of time it has been absorbed and is now as much a part of the essence of the country as the lochs and mountains, literature, arts, science, engineering and inventions.

## THE **10** ESSENTIALS

*If you only have a short time to visit Scotland, or would like to get a really complete picture of the country, here are the essentials:*

*Magnificent red sandstone remains of the Cistercian Abbey of Melrose*

• **Sample malt whisky**. There are so many varieties to choose from, but try the peaty taste of Islay Bowmore and the smooth, almost velvet quality of Grants Balvenie.

• **Drive the coast road from Ayr to Girvan**. Look out to Arran, Kintyre, the craggy rock of Ailsa Craig and, on a clear day, the coastline of Ireland.

• **Ride the train from Inverness to Kyle of Lochalsh**. This is one of the most scenic rail routes in Britain, particularly from the special observation cars.

• **Go to a pub music session**. The finest traditional Scottish music is found in informal pub sessions. Try the Scotia Bar in Glasgow (► 113).

• **Eat haggis, neeps and tatties**. Scotland's national dish is on the menu in many pubs and restaurants. Wash it down with a wee dram of whisky.

• **Go to a village gala**. Most small villages have a gala day with street parades, crowning of the Gala Queen, outdoor activities and a ceilidh in the village hall.

• **Visit one of the great abbey ruins in the South**. Even in ruins these are awesome. See Jedburgh and Melrose in the Borders or Dundrennan and Sweetheart in Dumfries and Galloway.

• **Visit the Museum of Scotland**. Opened in January 1999, this tells Scotland's story from the geological creation of the land to 20th-century industry.

• **Visit Glasgow's Barras**. Listen to the patter of the vendors at this famous flea market in the east end.

• **Visit Edinburgh Castle**. If you see only one thing, it has to be this. Then walk down the historic Royal Mile to the Palace of Holyroodhouse and the new Scottish Parliament.

*What could be better than a taste of haggis washed down with a wee dram?*

# The Shaping of Scotland

**2000 BC**
Early Pictish peoples settle the land and live by farming, hunting and fishing.

**AD 80–142**
The Romans make Hadrian's Wall the final frontier of the Roman Empire.

**9th–12th century**
Kenneth MacAlpin (c 843–58) and Duncan I (1034–40) are among the first kings of Scotland, while David I (1124–53) organises the state and the establishment of the great abbeys.

**1292–1314**
**The Scottish Wars of Independence**
John Balliol becomes king with the support of Edward I of England in

1292. When he allies with France, Edward crushes him at Dunbar. William Wallace wages a guerilla campaign, leading the Scots to victory at the Battle of Stirling Bridge (1297), only to be defeated at the Battle of Falkirk (1298). He is finally betrayed in 1305 and executed in London. Robert Bruce is crowned king in 1307 and defeats the English at Bannockburn in 1314.

**1544–5**
**'The Rough Wooing'**
Henry VIII tries to force the betrothal of his infant son to the infant Mary, Queen of Scots, by a series of border raids. This drives the Scots back towards the Auld Alliance with France.

*Wallace's historic defeat of the English at Stirling Bridge in 1297*

Mary is betrothed to the Dauphin and sent to France in 1548. In 1560, the Reformation is declared and papal authority renounced. Mary returns to Scotland after the death of her husband, clashes with John Knox, the Protestant reformer, and is implicated in the death of her husband, Lord Darnley. When she finally flees to England, she is imprisoned by Elizabeth I and executed in 1587.

**1603**
Mary's son, James VI, already King of Scotland, succeeds Elizabeth to the English throne. The Stuart dynasty is divided

*Mary, Queen of Scots*

by religious differences under Charles I and Charles II  The throne is offered to William of Orange in 1690.

**1707**
Tensions between the parliaments of Scotland and England lead to the Union of Parliaments, effectively abolishing the Scottish parliament.

**1715 and 1745**
Support for the cause of the Stuart claimant James VII of Scotland (James II of England) leads to Jacobite risings. The first, in 1715, is fuelled by the accession of George I and resentments against the Union, while the second, in 1745, is led by Bonnie Prince Charlie, who is defeated at Culloden in 1746.

**Early 19th century**
The landowners in the Highlands evict families and raze their houses to make way for profitable sheep. The Highlands are emptied of people, some to the newly industrial lowlands, while others emigrate to the New World.

**20th century**
Government becomes more democratic and suffrage is extended to women. The rise of the trade union movement, together with rent strikes and the socialist campaigner John MacLean, gain Glasgow the reputation as Red Clydeside. The founding of the Scottish Nationalist Party in 1928 indicates a resurgence in the desire for self determination which has ebbed and flowed over the century. After the referendum for a Scottish Parliament in 1998, Donald Dewar, the Scottish Secretary declares, 'There shall be a Scottish Parliament – I like that.'

**1 July 1999**
The Scottish Parliament reopens after nearly 300 years.

*The new Scottish Parliament's temporary home on Edinburgh's Mound*

# Peace & Quiet

There are many sparsely populated areas of Scotland where the tranquillity seeps into you. You can walk through forests and over moors and mountains without seeing a single other person and on the top of some of the hills you could truly believe you were the last person on earth. On uninhabited islands, in the wild flow country (ancient peat bogs) of the north or in the pastoral landscapes in the Borders, it is easy to enjoy the solitude.

*Family walking on a rocky trail by a burbling burn in Arran*

## Water

Scotland is surrounded by sea, and on remote Shetland or the Mull of Galloway you can find long stretches of isolated beaches or rocky coves with not a soul in sight. Although Dundee is a busy town, just a few miles away you will find the sandy beach of Broughty Ferry. There are always people there, walking their dogs, picking up shells or driftwood or gazing out over the broad calm waters of the Tay, but it's an agreeable companionship as you smile and pass by. In many cities, and across the industrial heart-lands, there are the historic byways of old canals such as the Union Canal in Edinburgh, now converted to leisure activities, where you can walk or cycle on the towpath or take a slow boat to nowhere along a tree-lined corridor behind the city streets. In the hills, moorlands and mountains of Scotland you can always hear the sound of rushing burns, tumbling over stones down rocky steps, or, hidden at the foot of a glen, a river winding gently down into some still reflective loch.

## Parks and Forests

In countryside or city, you are never far from pleasant parkland or forest trails. Glasgow, known as the 'Dear Green Place' because of its extensive parks, has Glasgow Green at its very heart. Edinburgh is a city full of gardens. At the bottom of the Royal Mile, through Dunbar Close, there is a secret little 17th-century garden, with herb gardens and stone seats, where you can escape from the hurly-burly to a tiny green haven. There are vast areas of forest everywhere in Scotland, many of them with way-

marked forest trails. There can be nothing more calming than walking through miles of forest, suddenly emerging at the top of a hill with a glorious view or finding ancient bridges or Celtic crosses by the wayside. There are several way-marked forest walks around the lovely village of Dunkeld in Perthshire; you can walk by the rivers and find the old Birnam oak, a sole survivor of the ancient Caledonian forest or the 65m Douglas fir and enormous cedar of Lebanon on the Hermitage woodland walk.

Above: the clifftop path from Portpatrick to Dunskey Castle
Below: the Hermitage Bridge near Dunkeld

## Churches

In Dunkeld you can visit Dunkeld Cathedral, and there are many churches, abbeys and sacred places all over the country in which you can find solace and a quiet retreat. From the great Border abbeys and the lovely medieval gem of Rosslyn Chapel to the perfect little Italian chapel created by the POWs in Orkney and the standing stones of Callanish, there are places of ritual and prayer for quiet and reflective contemplation.

# Scotland's Famous

### Robert Burns

One of the world's greatest poets was born in Alloway, near Ayr, in 1759. Robert Burns was greatly influenced by the singing and story-telling of his mother, Agnes Broun. He became a celebrity after the publication of his first volume of poems, *The Kilmarnock Edition*, was feted by Edinburgh society, and travelled throughout Scotland. After an unsuccessful farming venture at Ellisland in Dumfriesshire, he obtained a commission as an Excise man in Dumfries where he continued until his untimely death in 1796. Single-handed, he rescued and preserved the core of the Scottish song tradition through his work on Johnstone's Scots Musical Museum.

*Robert Burns, Scotland's Bard*

**Auld Lang Syne**
Academics argue that the hand of Burns is evident in *Auld Lang Syne*. He *did* rework many old songs, but he never claimed it of this one. Burns described it as 'the old Song of the olden times, which has never been in print, nor even in manuscript, untill I took it down from an old man's singing.'

### Mary, Queen of Scots

Mary is one of Scotland's most romantic characters. Queen of Scots from the age of six, she was betrothed to the Dauphin of France, and raised as a Frenchwoman. Following the Dauphin's death she returned to rule Scotland in 1561. At 18, effectively a foreigner in her own country, Mary clung to her Catholic religion, incurring the wrath of the misogynist Protestant reformer John Knox. Her reign was short and tragic, clouded by intrigue, suspicion and murder. Eventually defeated, she fled to England where, after a long imprisonment, she was beheaded at Fotheringay in 1587.

### William Wallace

Wallace, a shadowy historical figure, was born at Ellerslie in Ayrshire. He won a remarkable victory against a vastly superior English force at the Battle of Stirling Bridge in 1297. Created Guardian of Scotland, he recaptured Berwick but was eventually betrayed by the perfidious Scottish nobility. He was hung, drawn and quartered at Tyburn, London, in 1305.

### Sir Sean Connery

Sean Thomas Connery was born in Edinburgh in 1930. His big break came in 1962 when he was cast as Secret Agent James Bond. He won an Oscar in 1987 and was later voted the World's Sexiest Man. Connery is a passionate supporter of the Scottish National Party.

# Top Ten

Above: *medieval stained glass from Sir William Burrell's amazing art collection*
Right: *a Scottish piper, a sight often seen on the streets of Edinburgh*

# 1
# Burns National Heritage Park

54B3

Alloway

01292 443700

Apr–Oct, daily 9–6 (5 in winter). Burns Cottage closes at 4 in winter

Restaurant (£)

Hourly bus Ayr to Alloway. Western 57

Nearest train station Ayr

Very good

Moderate

Culzean Castle and Country Park (► 53)

*View of the Burns Monument and River Doon from the bridge where Tam o'Shanter escaped the witches*

*Alloway was Robert Burns' birthplace and the setting for his well-loved poem of ghosts and witches* Tam o' Shanter.

Robert Burns' father, William Burnes, built his 'auld clay biggin' near the banks of the River Doon, with walls 1m thick and tiny windows to protect against the chill Scottish winters. This long, low, thatched cottage, where Robert was born, still stands today, restored to its original condition, at the centre of the Burns National Heritage Park. Among the fascinating memorabilia on display are a plaster cast of the poet's skull, his Bible, and various original manuscripts, including the world's most famous song of parting *Auld Lang Syne*.

The manuscript of *Tam o' Shanter*, also on view in the cottage, is translated into virtual reality at the nearby visitors' centre in the Tam o' Shanter Experience. This hilarious and atmospheric tale recounts how the hapless Tam, in a drunken stupor, blunders upon the witches, then entranced by the pretty young Nannie, roars out, 'Weel done Cutty sark!', only to be chased from Alloway Kirk to the Brig o' Doon by a 'hellish legion' of witches. The reality of 'Alloway's auld haunted kirk' is close by and in this eerie ruin it is easy to imagine the open coffins and malignant tokens of the poem. Follow the chase from here to the Brig o' Doon, where Tam's mare Meg lost her tail to the winsome witch. This narrow old stone bridge was on the main road from Ayr to Carrick, a route well trodden by Burns, and gives some idea of the primitive state of Scotland's roads 200 years ago.

# 2
# Burrell Collection

*This wonderful museum is built around an
exquisite, idiosyncratic collection, gathered over a
period of 80 years.*

The Rehearsal, *by Degas,
from the Burrell
Collection*

The millionaire shipping magnate Sir William Burrell left his
eclectic collection of paintings, tapestries, stained glass,
furniture, silver and precious objects of all kinds to the
people of Glasgow in 1944. He was a magpie who started
collecting as a boy and continued until his death in 1958,
by which time his acquisitions numbered some 8,000
treasures and artefacts from around the world.

For years the collection lay in dusty storerooms until the
present building in Pollok Country Park was constructed in
1983 to house it, enhancing it and adorned by it. This red
sandstone, wood and glass structure nestles in a corner of
the parkland next to a grove of chestnut and sycamore.
Inside, the great glass walls bring the woodlands into the
heart of the museum. Medieval stone doorways and
windows have been built into the fabric of the building,
antique stained glass hangs before the glass walls and the
rooms are clad in ancient tapestries. Three rooms from
Burrell's home at Hutton Castle have been re-created with
their windows looking out on to the glass-roofed central
courtyard. The collection is particularly strong on rare
oriental porcelain and fine medieval French tapestries, but
includes paintings by Cezanne and Degas and sculptures
by Rodin. It is intriguing not just for the objects and the
building but because of the man who assembled it.

46A1

Pollok Country Park,
Glasgow

0141 287 2699

Mon–Thu and Sat, 10–5,
Fri and Sun from 10

Restaurant (££)

45, 48A and 57 from the
centre of Glasgow

Pollokshaws West

Very good

Free

# 3
# Culloden Battlefield

✚ 79D3

✉ 10km (6 miles) east of Inverness

☎ 01463 790607

🕓 Moor always open. Visitors' centre daily 9–5:30 (10–4 in winter). Closed Jan

🚌 Country Buses, Bluebird Buses from Inverness

♿ Good

✋ Cheap

↔ Cawdor Castle (➤ 80), Fort George (➤ 81)

*Old Leanach Cottage, as it was on 16 April, 1746, at the Battle of Culloden*

*This desolate moor, where the last battle on British soil was fought, was the scene of savage slaughter after the defeat of the Jacobites.*

This bleak moorland has been restored to the condition it was in on that fateful morning in 1746 when the hopes of the Royal House of Stuart to regain the throne of Scotland were forever dashed. It is a melancholy site where, tradition has it, the birds never sing and where no heather grows on the graves of the clansmen slaughtered in the aftermath by the forces of the Duke of Cumberland.

The broad, windswept expanse of Culloden Moor was ideal for the government's cavalry and artillery – the entrenched guns laid waste the Highland ranks. When finally the Highlanders charged, they became bogged down in the mud and scattered in disorder. Their infantry, already outnumbered, exhausted and starving after the long march from Derby, faltered and fell under a murderous hail of shot. The wounded survivors were slaughtered where they lay, and indiscriminate butchery of men, women and children was encouraged by Cumberland on the road to Inverness. The following year, all weapons, bagpipes, tartan and the kilt were banned by law in a bid to destroy the Highland culture and the clan system. Today, the episode is described in an excellent audio-visual in the visitor centre.

The Battle of Culloden was the last battle of the Jacobite rebellion of 1745, and the final defeat was followed by savage cruelty and years of persecution. An oppressive sadness and poignancy surrounds the memorial cairns, the sort of atmosphere that clings to such places as the Somme and Auschwitz which have witnessed pitiless waste of human life.

# 4
# Edinburgh Castle

*Home to monarchs, scene of banquets and siege, this castle is not only at the heart of Scotland's capital but of its history.*

Edinburgh Castle dominates the city from every angle and is visible from miles away. Over a million people visit every year and the queues for the Crown Room start to form early every day. The ancient Honours of Scotland are the oldest crown jewels in Europe, and the Stone of Destiny on which all Scots monarchs were crowned is also on view here.

There's been a fortification on this great volcanic rock since Celtic times, and the tiny Norman St Margaret's Chapel, the oldest building in Edinburgh, has stood intact for more than 900 years. The newly restored Royal Apartments include the room where Mary, Queen of Scots gave birth to the future James VI of Scotland (James I of England). The Great Hall has seen many historic gatherings and is still used for receptions by the Scottish First Minister. In the castle's cellar is the colossal cannon called Mons Meg, which fired its massive stone cannon-balls at the Battle of Flodden in 1513, a devastating defeat for the Scots by the English. At 1PM you can witness the firing of the one o'clock gun – not Mons Meg! The custom, which dates back to an era when few people owned clocks or watches, distinguishes the residents from the visitors. Visitors are often startled, Edinburgh folk just check their watches.

In August, the Castle Esplanade is the venue for the world-famous Edinburgh Military Tattoo. For three weeks the Army presents a dramatic, floodlit programme of music, marching and historical re-enactments. Almost as impressive as the castle itself are the views of the city of Edinburgh and surrounding countryside from its ramparts.

➕ 34C2

✉ At the top of the Royal Mile

☎ 0131 225 9846

🕐 Apr–Sep, daily 9:30–6 (5 in winter)

🚇 Waverley

♿ Poor

✋ Expensive

↔ Grassmarket and Museum of Scotland (➤ 32), Palace of Holyroodhouse and People's Story (➤ 33), Princes Street Gardens and the Scottish Parliament (➤ 36)

*Edinburgh Castle, spectacularly set atop its volcanic crag*

# 5
# Glen Coe

✚ 78C2

✉ 24km (15 miles) south of Fort William

🍴 Snack bar in Glencoe Village (£)

🚌 Highland Country Buses from Fort William; Scottish City Link from Glasgow and Fort William

*Buachaille Etive Beag, the Small Shepherd of Etive, looks down on Lochan na Fol, Glen Coe*

*This majestic mountain pass running from Glencoe village to Rannoch Moor is one of the most spectacular and desolate sights in Scotland.*

Lying at the foot of massive mountains, often disappearing into heavy swirling cloud, the gloom in Glen Coe can be oppressive. Under clear blue skies, the smooth green humps of the mountains, the rocky summits of the Three Sisters, the wide floor of the glen and the distant mountain tops beyond are a familiar sight the world over on calendars and in films. *Braveheart*, *Restless Natives*, *Highlander* and many other movies were shot in the Glen.

There is an awesome stillness about the Glen, which even the great numbers of tourists, walkers and climbers never disturb. However, its peace was rudely shattered on a winter morning over 300 years ago when Glen Coe became a byword for treachery. The chief of the Clan

MacDonald was late in swearing allegiance to the Crown. Campbell of Glenlyon, under orders signed by King William, took his men to Glencoe to make an example of the MacDonalds. He billeted his men there on the pretext that they were just passing through. In the early dawn of 13 February, 1692, throughout the glen the Campbells dragged MacDonald men from their beds and murdered them, burning the houses as they went. The women, some carrying infants, fled into the mountains in a piercing snow storm, many perishing miserably.

Nowadays the unpredictable weather still claims lives among the skiers, walkers and climbers who flock to the Glen. There are countless challenging walks and climbs, but this is no land for a casual afternoon stroll.

In summer a trip up the ski lift to the summit will be rewarded by spectacular views over Rannoch Moor and the surrounding mountains.

Above: *the steep snow-covered slopes of Glen Coe are very popular with skiers*

# 6
# New Lanark

54C4

In a gorge below Lanark

01555 661345

Daily 11–5

Tea room (£)

Bus service from station in Lanark

Lanark

Horsemarket, Ladyacre Road, Lanark ☎ 01555 661661

Good

Moderate

*Robert Owen built his New Lanark spinning mills on the banks of the River Clyde*

*New Lanark was the first example of a working environment planned to consider the welfare of the workforce as well as efficiency and profit.*

This was Robert Owen's utopian village, built near the Falls of Clyde to harness the power of the water for driving the cotton mills. New Lanark was much more than a mill town, it was a model village and Owen (1771–1858) was the forerunner of the great Victorian philanthropists who built towns such as Saltaire and Port Sunlight. Contrary to the wisdom of the time, Owen believed that a happy workforce would be a productive workforce, so he provided modern housing, a shop, a school and recreation facilities. His employees also worked shorter hours and had better working conditions, schooling was compulsory and he did not employ children under 10 in the mill.

His competitors thought he was crazy and that his business would suffer. They were astonished when it became more profitable rather than less. New Lanark survived as a mill town into the 20th century and was saved from ultimate demolition when it was restored as a conservation project. You can tour the houses, gardens and recreation hall, see the restored looms working and learn about life at the time through the eyes of a young girl in the Annie McLeod Experience.

Although it is in the industrial heartland of Scotland, New Lanark is set in a rural location on the banks of the Clyde. This was part of Owen's plan that his workers should live in pleasant surroundings. You can follow the delightful riverside walk to the Falls of Clyde to appreciate the importance of this.

# 7
# Rosslyn Chapel

*This tiny, atmospheric, medieval chapel is an exquisite masterpiece of the mason's art, with an unrivalled range and delicacy of carving.*

Rosslyn Chapel with the famed Apprentice Pillar on the left

Rosslyn Chapel is possibly the most mysterious building in Scotland, like a great medieval cathedral in miniature. It is richly carved, including the most complete *danse macabre* (dance of death) in Europe and, if you know where to look, you will see the death mask of King Robert the Bruce, reproduced in stone. Built by Sir William St Clair, it has strong connections with the Knights Templar, a mystical order of wealthy warrior monks, who fought with Robert the Bruce at Bannockburn (1314). They were credited with finding the Holy Grail and the treasures of Solomon.

It is said that the Holy Grail is hidden in the Apprentice Pillar, one of two great pillars. The story goes that the apprentice saw the pillar in a dream and carved it in his master's absence. The master was so angry and jealous when he saw the delicate and complicated work that he felled the apprentice with a single blow of his mallet. The master was hanged, and his effigy and that of the apprentice and his mother can be found close to the pillars. Whatever the truth of the legends, there is no doubt that the master masons who chiselled these intricate patterns and medieval likenesses from stone were exceptionally gifted.

Whether it is the medieval faces peering out of the stone on all sides or the 20 knights in full armour interred below, there is an eerie supernatural feel to this tiny chapel and a strange chill as you enter the crypt. A former curator once saw the apparition of a monk kneeling before the altar with four spectral knights standing guard over him.

✚ 55D4

✉ Off Chapel Loan, opposite The Roslin Glen Hotel, Roslin (11.6km/7 miles south of Edinburgh)

☎ 0131 440 2159

🕐 Mon–Sat 10–5, Sun noon–4:45

🍴 Coffee shop (£)

🚌 315 from Edinburgh (First Lowland)

✋ Moderate

# 8
# Skara Brae

✚ 29C4

✉ 13km (8 miles) north of Stromness, Orkney

☎ 01856 841815

🕐 Mon–Sat 9:30–6:30, Sun 2–6:30 (4:30 in winter)

✋ Moderate

*On a beautiful sandy sea-shore on the edge of the world is the perfectly preserved neolithic settlement of Skara Brae in Orkney.*

Buried for centuries under the sand dunes of the Bay of Skail, a great storm in 1850 uncovered this complete Stone Age village which has been extensively excavated.

The villagers dug holes into the sandy soil so that their homes were half underground affording some protection against the winds. Interconnecting passages between the huts were lined with sandstone slabs. Wandering around the site and looking down into these homes is a poignant experience. The layout of the rooms resembles any small peasant dwelling – except that everything is made of stone. The dresser is a couple of flagstone shelves resting on stone 'legs', the bed is three slabs of stone set against the wall to form a 'box', and there is a central hearth.

There are few trees on Orkney, which is why these ancient people had to use alternative materials. Whale jawbones were probably used as rafters to support the roof, tools (displayed in the visitors' centre) were made of bone and stone, and pottery was richly decorated. They were farmers who bred cows and sheep and grew cereals, they walked on this ground, and looking into their homes, their lives seem vivid and close. An excellent reconstruction of one of the stone houses, complete with roof, is well worth a visit.

*An early dwelling at Skara Brae Stone Age settlement on Orkney*

# 9
# The Tenement House, Glasgow

*Most of the population of industrial Scotland in the 19th and early 20th centuries lived in four- or five-storey tenement buildings similar to this one.*

Miss Agnes Toward moved into this three-roomed flat with her mother in 1911 and lived there until her death in 1965. Houses in tenements ranged from the single end, which would nowadays be called a studio flat, to apartments such as this one, with several bedrooms and even a bathroom. Most flats had no inside toilet but several families would share one toilet off the stairs. Better classes of tenement building were distinguished by the 'wally close', with ornate patterned ceramic tiles on the walls of the entry.

The kitchen of a tenement flat, with the cooking range for warmth, was the centre of family life. Miss Toward's kitchen utensils lie on the deal (fir or pine) table, her jars of home-made jam are still sealed above, the washboard is in the deep ceramic sink and the washing hangs to dry on the pulley. The bed, built into the recess in the kitchen, consists of a lumpy mattress on boards and snow-white bed linen, and there is a another bed tucked away below to accommodate the large families which were the norm.

When Miss Toward died it was discovered that she had never thrown anything away. She had kept bus tickets, letters booking her holidays, even newspapers, which were piled high on chairs and tables. It was a treasure trove of ephemera, portraying a way of life that was passing, a tiny fragment of history caught in amber, and nostalgia for those who can remember it.

46B4

145 Buccleuch Street, Glasgow

0141 333 0183

Mar–Oct, daily 2–5

From Buchanan Street Bus Station

Charing Cross

Moderate

Glasgow School of Art (► 48)

*Victorian middle-class parlour in Miss Toward's Tenement House*

# 10
# Traquair House

> *Dating from the early 12th century, Traquair claims to be the oldest continually inhabited house in Scotland.*

✚ 55D3

✉ 2km (1½ miles) south of Innerleithen

☎ 01896 830323

🕐 Daily Jun–Aug, 10:30–5:30; Apr, May, Sep, 12:30–5:30; Oct, Fri–Sun 12:30–5:30

🍴 Tea room (£)

🚌 62 from Edinburgh and Peebles to Innerleithen

✋ Expensive

The house was originally built as a hunting lodge for the Scottish kings and queens. Because of its strategic position on the banks of the River Tweed, it was fortified against border raids. James III gave it to his court musician, who sold it to the Earl of Buchan for £3 15s. Buchan's son James Stuart became the first laird, and from then on it developed as a family home. The main block was completed around 1600 and another two wings were added a century later. The famous Bear Gates were erected in 1737 at a cost of £12 15s for the pillars, £10 4s for the carving of the stone bears and four gallons of ale for the workmen. The gates opened into a long tree-lined avenue which Prince Charles Edward Stuart trod one late autumn day in 1745 as he set off on his ill-fated venture to try and reclaim the throne for the House of Stuart. The Earl swore that they would never be opened again until a Stuart returned to the throne of Scotland. To this day they remain sealed.

The extensive woodlands and gardens around Traquair are usually buzzing with activity – there are various craft workshops and a brewery. The beer is brewed in the old brew-house and fermented in the original 200-year-old oak casks. The maze next to the house is a delight for children of all ages, while the house itself is a labyrinth, with lots of quirky little steps and corridors and secret passages. Above all, it still has the feel of a family home.

*Traquair House – a fine fortified Borders' castle*

# What to See

Above: *Balmoral was built for Queen Victoria in 1855*
Right: *a champion haggis-maker with his wares*

27

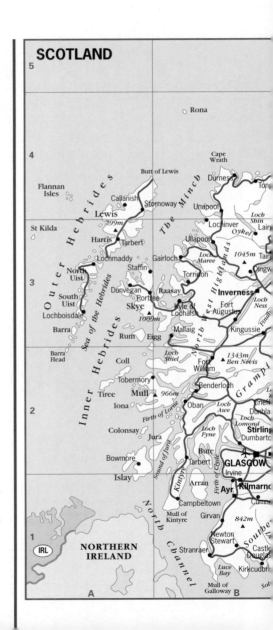

## SCOTLAND

5

○ Rona

4

Cape Wrath

Butt of Lewis

Durness

Tong

Flannan Isles

Callanish

Stornoway

The Minch

Unapool

Loch Shin

St Kilda

Lewis

799m

Lochinver

Oykel

Lair

Harris

Tarbert

Ullapool

Loch Maree

1045m

Tain

Lochmaddy

Gairloch

Dingw

North Uist

Staffin

Torridon

Inverness

3

South Uist

Dunvegan

Raasay

Portree

Skye

Kyle of Lochalsh

Fort Augustus

Loch Ness

Lochboisdale

1009m

Findh

Barra

Mallaig

Kingussie

Sea of the Hebrides

Rum

Eigg

Loch Shiel

North West Highlands

Barra Head

Coll

Fort William

1343m Ben Nevis

Inner Hebrides

Tobermory

Benderloch

Grampi

2

Tiree

Mull

966m

L

Iona

Firth of Lorne

Oban

Loch Awe

Crief

Dunbla

Colonsay

Jura

Loch Fyne

Loch Lomond

Stirling

Dumbarto

Bowmore

Bute

Tarbert

GLASGOW

Islay

Sound of Jura

Kintyre

Firth of Clyde

Irvine

Arran

Kilmarno

Ayr

Campbeltown

Cumn

North

Mull of Kintyre

Girvan

842m

1

IRL

Newton Stewart

Southe

NORTHERN IRELAND

Channel

Stranraer

Castle Douglas

Luce Bay

Kirkcudbri

Mull of Galloway

Sol

A

B

Orkney
Islands                    Fair Isle

Westray
Rousay          Sanday
kara Brae       Stronsay
tromness  Maes Howe
          Kirkwall
            Italian Chapel
Hoy       South
          Ronaldsay
Pentland Firth
          Duncansby
          Head
Thurso

Wick

Helmsdale

ornoch
Firth
ray Firth
    Elgin    Banff      Kinnaird
                        Head
lairn    Keith          Fraserburgh
        Spey
        Inverurie       Peterhead

viemore      Don
09m   o u n t a i n s   Aberdeen
      Dee
      Braemar          Stonehaven

Pitlochry
      Forfar       Montrose
Dundee          Arbroath
  Perth    Firth of Tay
Kinross    St Andrews
unfermline  Firth of Forth
alkirk    Kirkcaldy
        Dunbar      St Abb's Head
oatbridge  EDINBURGH   Eyemouth
Peebles  Galashiels  Tweed
plands    Jedburgh  Coldstream
    Hawick    The Cheviot Hills

Dumfries
Gretna
Green
        ENGLAND

Shetland
Islands              Unst
              Yell
                    Fetlar
Hillswick
St Magnus Bay        Whalsay
Sandness
              Bressay
  Foula    Lerwick
  Scalloway  Broch of
            Mousa
Jarlshof  Sumburgh
          Head

  Fair Isle

0  20  40  60  80  100 km
0    20    40    60 miles

C                    D

# Edinburgh & the Borders

Built on a series of volcanic rocks, Scotland's capital is undoubtedly one of the most beautiful cities of Europe. Few sights can compare with Princes Street Gardens laid out beneath the castle, massive on its dark crag of volcanic rock.

During the many wars with England, Edinburgh Castle was often the destination of the English armies and the area between the castle and the border was laid waste time and again. Even in times of peace, cross-border raids by cattle reivers (thieves) meant that the inhabitants of this region could never relax, but it was also an area of prosperity. Huge castles, built for defence, became grand dwellings of the aristocracy in times of peace. As you drive, cycle or walk through the rolling hills of the borders or along the rivers Yarrow, Tweed and Ettrick, the tranquillity belies its violent past.

*'There's Gala Water,*
*Leader Haughs, both lying*
*right before us; and*
*Dryburgh, where with*
*chiming Tweed, the*
*Lintwhites sing in chorus.'*

WILLIAM WORDSWORTH
1803

————————●————————

*Top-notch social history museum in Edinburgh's Canongate Tolbooth*

# Edinburgh

**Edinburgh is a city of two towns. Beside the castle are the narrow closes, winding streets and tall tenements of the Old Town, while opposite are the elegant classical squares, broad streets and peaceful gardens of the Georgian New Town. It's a joy to walk around this rich architectural tapestry, to stroll through gardens where suddenly the city bustle disappears into greenery and birdsong, or to climb the many hills and capture a glimpse of the Firth of Forth or majestic Arthur's Seat, and another perspective of this incomparable city.**

## What to See in Edinburgh

### BRITANNIA                                       ✪✪✪

Since the former royal yacht *Britannia* opened to the public at the Port of Leith in 1998, it has become Edinburgh's second-biggest attraction after the castle. There is an excellent visitors' centre with exhibits of photographs and reconstructed crews' cabins, but the real enticement is the yacht itself. You can peep into the Queen's bedroom, the royal sitting rooms and into various magnificently furnished state rooms which have witnessed momentous international receptions.

➕ 35E4

✉ Ocean Drive, Leith
☎ 0131 555 8800
🕐 Daily 10:30–6
🍴 Excellent café on premises (£
♿ Moderate
❓ Pre-booking recommended ☎ 0131 555 5566

### CALTON HILL                                     ✪✪✪

Calton Hill is a superb vantage point from which to view the city, the Firth of Forth and the kingdom of Fife beyond. On Friday evenings you can also see the stars as the City Observatory is open to the public. The remainder of the buildings on Calton Hill are curious structures – the Nelson Monument is a telescope-shaped tower, while the uncompleted Greek temple is the National Monument to those killed in the Napoleonic Wars.

➕ 35E4
🍴 Excellent restaurants near by (£–£££)

### EDINBURGH CASTLE (➤ 19, TOP TEN)

### GRASSMARKET

Edinburgh's first market area built outside the city walls has seen many changes over the years. From market-place to public execution site, it became a depressed slum area, frequented by down-and-outs. Recently, its fortunes have revived and it is now a cosmopolitan centre with an eclectic mix of shops and pubs. TV personality Clarissa Dickson Wright of *Two Fat Ladies* fame runs the Cook's Book Shop on the corner, while across the road, Stan Wood, Britain's only commercial palaeontologist, has his fossil shop. Along the brightly coloured façades in Victoria Street are a brush shop, a traditional cheesemonger, a French baker and an incredible indoor flea market called Byzantium.

### MUSEUM OF SCOTLAND ✪✪✪

Edinburgh's latest addition merges a bold modern design with the vaulted hall, cast-iron balconies and glass roof of the Royal Museum of Scotland to which is is adjoined. Displays are built into the walls, and by the tantalising use of arches and gaps, discrete spaces are created. Unlike the Royal Museum, which in true Victorian style has a wonderful miscellaneous selection of exhibits and curiosities ranging from across the globe, the new museum focuses on Scotland. The whole of Scotland's story, from prehistoric rocks and fossils to the late 20th century unfolds here. One of the more gruesome displays is the early Scottish guillotine, the Iron Maiden, along with the names of some of those who lost their heads to it. Among the exhibits in the display of 20th-century items representative of the century is a Fender Stratocaster guitar, chosen by the Prime Minister, Tony Blair.

---

**🏁 34C2**

**🍴** Excellent cafés (£) and restaurants on the square

**❓** Lot of nightlife, geared mainly to students and young people

---

**🏁 35D2**

**✉** Chambers Street

**☎** 0131 225 7534/247 4219

**🕐** Mon–Sat 10–5 (Tue until 8), Sun noon–5

**🍴** Excellent café (£) and high-class restaurant (£££) on premises

**♿** Moderate (free Tue 4:30–8). Ticket also covers Royal Museum of Scotland

*The most colourful and eclectic collection of shops in Edinburgh is here in Victoria Street*

## PALACE OF HOLYROODHOUSE

At the bottom of the spine of volcanic rock known as the Royal Mile sits Holyroodhouse Palace, home of Scottish monarchs since the 16th century, although most of the current building dates from 1671. It was here that Mary, Queen of Scots, spent much of her short, tragic reign, and

where she suffered the bigoted tirades of John Knox and witnessed the savage slaughter of her servant Riccio. Holyrood is the Queen's official residence in Scotland, but the state and historic apartments are open to the public.

Spreading out behind the palace, **Holyrood Park** is a wide open space dominated by the great volcanic plug known as Arthur's Seat. A climb to the top is rewarded with stunning views of Edinburgh, the kingdom of Fife and the Borders, and there are plenty of paths for less strenuous walking or cycling. Rock climbers and abseilers can practise their skills on Salisbury Crags, while the less energetic can just picnic by the pond. It is particularly peaceful on Sundays when cars are prohibited.

## THE PEOPLE'S STORY

Situated in the former Canongate Tolbooth on the Royal Mile, this fascinating free museum of social history is one of the gems of Edinburgh. Re-creations of living quarters, workshops and displays of artefacts seek to explain the manner and quality of life for ordinary Edinburgh folk over the years.

## PRINCES STREET

One of the great joys of shopping in Princes Street is the space. Only one side of the street has buildings, the other side is Princes Street Gardens (➤ 36), where you can escape the crowds. Jenner's, with its labyrinth of departments and tiers of polished balconies, is the world's oldest independent department store. If you tire of shopping, slip out the back door into Rose Street, which has more public houses than any other street in Scotland.

35F3
Bottom of Royal Mile
0131 556 7371
Apr–Oct, Mon–Sat 9:30–5:15, Sun 10–4:30; Nov–Mar, daily 9:30–3:45 (closed Good Fri, early May, early Jun and late Jun to mid-Jul, or when the Queen is in residence; telephone to check)
Excellent tea room (£) just up Royal Mile
Expensive

**Holyrood Park**
Open all hours
Excellent cafés/restaurants on the Royal Mile (£)

*Edinburgh fishwife in wax at the People's Story museum*

35E3
Canongate Tolbooth
0131 331 5545
Mon–Sat 10–5 (Sun 2–5 during Festival only)
Excellent cafe (£) across street  Free

34B3
Excellent cafés/bars in Rose Street (£££)

33

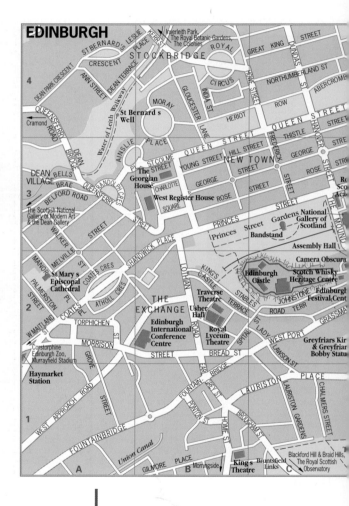

# EDINBURGH

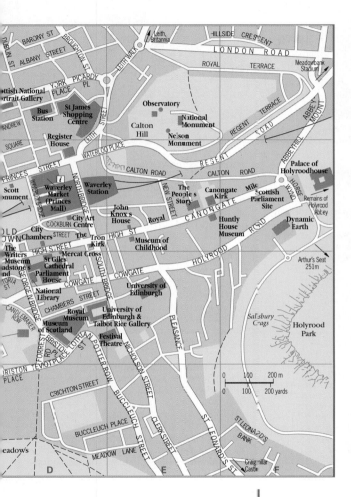

BARONY ST

Leith, Britannia

HILLSIDE CRESCENT

LONDON ROAD

DUBLIN ST

BROUGHTON ST

ALBANY STREET

ROYAL TERRACE

Meadowbank Stadium

YORK PICARDY PL

LEITH WALK

ottish National rtrait Gallery

PLACE

St James Shopping Centre

Observatory

Bus Station

ANDREW

Calton Hill

National Monument

REGENT TERRACE

ABBEY MOUNT

Register House

LEITH STREET

Nelson Monument

SQUARE

NORTH BRIDGE

WATERLOO PLACE

REGENT ROAD

ABBEYHILL

CALTON ROAD

PRINCES

STREET

CALTON ROAD

Palace of Holyroodhouse

Scott onument

i

Waverley Market (Princes Mall)

Waverley Station

NEW STREET

The People's Story

Canongate Kirk

Scottish Parliament Site

HORSE WYND

Remains of Holyrood Abbey

WAVERLEY BRIDGE

John Knox's House

Royal

CANONGATE

Mile

City Art Centre

COCKBURN STREET

Huntly House Museum

HOLYROOD ROAD

Dynamic Earth

OLD TOWN

City Chambers

HIGH ST

The Tron Kirk

Museum of Childhood

The Writers Museum adstone's nd

HIGH STREET

Mercat Cross

Arthur's Seat 251m

St Giles Cathedral

SOUTH BRIDGE

HOLYROOD

VICTORIA ST

Parliament House

COWGATE

GEORGE IV BRIDGE

National Library

University of Edinburgh

Salisbury Crags

CHAMBERS STREET

Holyrood Park

CANDLEMAKER ROW

Royal Museum Museum of Scotland

University of Edinburgh & Talbot Rice Gallery

PLEASANCE

FORREST RD

BRISTO PLACE

TEVIOT PLACE

Festival Theatre

LOTHIAN ST

RISTON PLACE

POTTER ROW

NICHOLSON STREET

0    100    200 m

0    100    200 yards

CRICHTON STREET

BUCCLEUGH STREET

eadows

BUCCLEUCH PLACE

CLERK STREET

ST LEONARD'S BANK

MEADOW LANE

ST LEONARD'S ST

Craigmillar Castle

D          E          F

*Princes Street Gardens are a delight at all seasons, but attract the crowds on a warm summer day*

### PRINCES STREET GARDENS ●●●

It is hard to believe that these carefully tended gardens were once the Nor' Loch ('north loch'), into which ran all the sewage of the Old Town. The gardens run the length of Princes Street, divided into two parts by the Mound, the pile of earth excavated when the New Town was built. The Greek splendour of the Royal Scottish Academy and the National Gallery of Scotland now occupy the site. Locals and visitors alike relax in the gardens, enjoying the flowers, admiring the famous Floral Clock, feeding the squirrels or simply sitting in the shade of a willow tree or on one of the polished wooden memorial benches. There's a bandstand for summer concerts and an open-air café. On the last night of the Festival, the spectacular Bank of Scotland Fireworks Concert is staged here, and at New Year it hosts the world's biggest Hogmanay (New Year's Eve) party.

### SCOTTISH NATIONAL PORTRAIT GALLERY ●

In a Gothic red sandstone building on Queen Street, this gallery offers a fascinating tour of the great and the good of Scotland past and present. Among the kings and queens in the collection are portraits of Mary, Queen of Scots, as well as her persecutor John Knox and her ill-fated husband Lord Darnley. Robert Burns, J M Barrie and Hugh McDiarmid are among the literary greats, and living subjects include the legendary accordionist Jimmy Shand.

### THE SCOTTISH PARLIAMENT ●●

After a break of nearly 300 years, Scotland again has its own Parliament. Since 1999 it has been in temporary accommodation in the Church of Scotland Assembly at the top of the Mound. Meanwhile, a futuristic new building is being built at the bottom of the Royal Mile adjacent to the Palace of Holyroodhouse and the Dynamic Earth exhibition (► 110). The Parliament shop and visitors' centre are at the corner of the Royal Mile and George IV Bridge.

# Edinburgh Walk

This walk takes in the Old Town of Edinburgh, including the historic Grassmarket, the Royal Mile and Greyfriars Church. The view from Calton Hill at sunset is spectacular.

*Begin on Castle Esplanade. At the end, turn down the steps to the Grassmarket. Cross Johnstone Terrace and continue to the bottom. Turn left along the Grassmarket.*

Investigate the colourful shops of Victoria Street to the left and return to the Grassmarket.

*Cross over into Candlemaker Row and go up to the statue of Greyfriars Bobby.*

To the right is Greyfriars Church, where the faithful little terrier, Greyfriars Bobby, kept vigil over his master's grave, and opposite is the Museum of Scotland (► 32).

*Turn left along George IV Bridge, then right down the Royal Mile.*

You will pass St Giles Cathedral, the Museum of Childhood and John Knox's House. Have a look at the Palace of Holyroodhouse at the bottom (► 33).

*Turn back up the Royal Mile to White Horse Close on the right. Go through it on to Calton Road. Turn left and take the steep steps on your right up to Regent Road. Cross and take the road leading up behind the Royal High School to Calton Hill.*

On the way up you will find a cairn dedicated to the achievement of a Scottish Parliament. On Calton Hill pass the National Monument and Nelson's Monument (► 31).

*Take the steps back to Regent Road. Turn right, cross the road and head towards Princes Street. After the Mound, enter Princes Street Gardens past the Floral Clock. Exit by the gate towards the castle and Ramsay Garden. Head up right through Ramsay Garden and return.*

**Distance**
6km (4 miles)

**Time**
2–6 hours

**Start/end point**
Castle Esplanade
✚ 28C2

**Lunch**
Clarinda's Tea Room
☎ 0131 557 1883

*Antonio David's portrait of Bonnie Prince Charlie, part of the collection at the National Portrait Gallery*

# In the Know

If you only have a short time to visit Scotland and would like to get a real flavour of the country, here are some ideas:

## 10
### Ways to Be a Local

**Ask for a pint and a hauf in a pub**. You'll get a pint of beer and a dram of whisky – not a pint and a half of beer.

**Listen to a piper or a pipe band**. This outdoor instrument stirs the blood of all true Scots.

**Visit a session of the Scottish Parliament**. The visitor centre at the top of the Royal Mile offers information about the parliament. Free tickets are available to watch the proceedings.

**Eat a fish supper** or a smoked sausage supper while sitting on a harbour wall, watching the boats.

**Drink Irn-Bru**. This sweet orange-coloured drink is the classic hangover cure and typifies the worst in Scottish preferences.

**Go for afternoon tea** in a village or church hall. These fund-raising events offer delicious home baking.

**Go for a sail 'doon the watter'**. Take a trip on the *Waverley*, the world's last ocean-going paddle steamer, from Glasgow to the Clyde resorts.

**Look for your name** in the lists of clan tartans. Many people have a tartan even if they don't realise that their name is Scottish.

*The silvery Tay has some of Scotland's best fishing*

**Read the *Sunday Post*** which is full of sentimental stories and Scottish kitsch, and is sent to exiled Scots all over the world. The best bits are the comic strips of *Oor Wullie* and *The Broons*.

**Go to a ceilidh** at a hotel or a village hall or at one of the many folk music festivals which take place in the summer.

## 10
### Good Places to Have Lunch

**The Ceilidh Place** ✉ West Argyll Street, Ullapool ☎ 01854 612103. Fresh bread, hearty soups, a good vegetarian option and home baking.

**The Garden Café** ✉ Lennoxlove ☎ 01620 822156. The lovely setting of Lennoxlove House and gardens (➤ 40) and imaginative menu make it a relaxing lunch experience.

**Henderson's** ✉ 94 Hanover Street, Edinburgh ☎ 0131 225 2131. Well-known vegetarian salad bar with usually four or five hot choices, changing throughout the day, with puddings to die for.

**Hubbub** ✉ Academy Street, Dumfries ☎ 01387 264600. Lots of different rolls with imaginative fillings and a limited choice of main course and vegetarian options. Eat in or take away.

**The Lemon Tree** ✉ 5 West North Street, Aberdeen ☎ 01224 642230. BBC Scotland broadcasts live shows from here. Good soups, vegetarian options and substantial basic fare.

**Monty's** ✉ 5 Mounthooly Street, Lerwick ☎ 01595 696555. Sophisticated dining in the evening, simple high-quality dishes at lunch time.

**Nardini's** ✉ The Promenade, Largs ☎ 01475 674555. Enormous '50s-style seaside café. The décor is pure nostalgia and the ice-cream is legendary.

*Tartan at MacNaughton's of Pitlochry*

**78, St Vincent Street** ✉ Glasgow ☎ 0141 248 7878. Imaginative, high-quality food. Fresh Scottish ingredients with continental flair and excellent service.

**Togs Café** ✉ 9 Templehill, Troon ☎ 01292 312868. Intimate art deco-style café, modernised in the 1950s with neon and Vitrolite. A reminder of the days when teenagers hugged a frothy coffee all evening and listened to Tommy Steele. Standard café food – bacon butties, chips and knickerbocker glories.

**Valvona and Crolla** ✉ Leith Walk, Edinburgh ☎ 0131 556 6066. A wonderful Italian delicatessen (fresh pestos, cheeses, olive oils, breads and wines) with a stylish café at the back.

## **10**

## Top Activities

**Climbing**. The Highlands is the main area for climbing, with Aviemore as the main centre; there are strenuous opportunities in the Southern Uplands.

**Walking** through hills, mountains, moorlands, forests, along way-marked long-distance footpaths (the West Highland Way, the Southern Upland Way), and marked walks in country parks and estates.

**Fishing**. For salmon and trout fishing get a day ticket from the appropriate private estate, angling club or local council. There is sea fishing at seaside resorts.

**Golf** is the national game. If you can't get on one of the championship courses try one of the municipal courses and private clubs that admit day visitors – Girvan, Ayrshire; Thornhill, Dumfriesshire; Strathaven, Lanarkshire; and the Gowf Club, Loudoun, near Galston, Ayrshire.

**Curling**, Scotland's other national game, is now an Olympic sport. Many towns and hotels have ice rinks and offer tuition. Dumfries Ice Bowl, the Magnum Leisure Centre, Irvine and the Aberdeen Beach Leisure Centre are a few.

**Bird-watching**. The many species which can be seen range from the ospreys at Grantown-or-Spey and puffins on Shetland to the Spitsbergen barnacle geese at Caerlaverock, Dumfries.

**Cycling** is a great way to tour Scotland. There has been a huge growth in cycle paths across the country and in many towns and cities, particularly Edinburgh.

**Watersports**. Sailing, canoeing, white-water rafting, water-skiing, swimming, windsurfing – you name it, Scotland has

it. Watersports centres include Loch Ken Watersports in Dumfriesshire, Raasay Outdoors Centre in Skye and Strathclyde Park.

**Bowling** attracts players of all ages. It's a summer pastime and many local clubs admit visitors.

**Shooting**. Thousands of acres of grouse moors are given over to this pastime. Clay pigeon shooting is much more fun and there are centres throughout Scotland.

## **10**

## Scottish Inventors

- John Logie Baird (television)
- Alexander Graham Bell (telephone)
- Sir James Simpson (anaesthetic)
- Charles Macintosh (waterproof coat)
- John Dunlop (pneumatic tyre)
- Kirkpatrick MacMillan (bicycle)
- John Loudon McAdam (tarmacadam)
- Robert Watson Watt (radar)
- James Dewar (vacuum flask)
- Alexander Fleming (penicillin)

## **10**

## Best Golf Courses

- St Andrews, Old Course
- Carnoustie
- Royal Troon
- Turnberry, Ailsa
- Turnberry, Arran
- Royal Dornoch
- Haggs Castle
- Old Prestwick
- Gullane
- Muirfield

## What to See in the Borders

+ 55E3
✉ 3km (2 miles) west of Melrose
☎ 01896 752043
🕐 Mid-Mar to Oct, daily 10–5 (Mar–May and Oct, Sun 2–5)
🍴 Tea room on premises (£)
♿ Moderate

### ABBOTSFORD HOUSE                    ●●

Sir Walter Scott (1771–1832) designed Abbotsford and lived there for the last 20 years of his life. The Scots Baronial design, with medieval towers and turrets, reflects his romantic side. The library, housing Scott's huge collection of rare books is light and airy and also displays his accumulation of bizarre Scottish memorabilia, from Bonnie Prince Charlie's hair to the crucifix carried by Mary, Queen of Scots, when she was beheaded.

+ 55E4

**Lennoxlove**
✉ 3km (2 miles) south of Haddington
☎ 01620 823720
🕐 Easter weekend–31 Oct, Wed and Thu 2–4:30 half hourly tours. Hourly Apr and Oct. Some Sat and Sun opening (call for times)
🍴 Clarissa Dickson Wright's Garden Café (£)
♿ Moderate

### HADDINGTON                    ●●

The historic town of Haddington, a mixture of broad tree-lined streets and medieval street plan, is an architectural delight. The High Street, with its lanes and closes and quaint shops, is fronted by the elegant Town House designed by William Adam. Near by is the classical frontage of Carlyle House. The childhood home of Jane Welsh Carlyle, wife of Thomas Carlyle, the Sage of Chelsea, is tucked away behind it. Around the corner lies Haddington House, the oldest house in town, complete with re-created 17th-century garden. Further on, the tranquil riverside walk leads to St Mary's Collegiate Church, steeped in historical significance. The marks of the bombardment by the English during the 'Rough Wooing'(▶ 10) are still visible. John Knox, the great Protestant reformer, preached here; the Lauderdale Aisle is an exquisite Episcopalian chapel; and two of the lovely stained-glass windows are by Sir Edward Burne-Jones.

Just beyond Haddington is **Lennoxlove**, set in 240ha of verdant woodlands. It appears to have grown in an endearing mixture of styles around a medieval tower and has a collection of furniture, paintings and mementoes of Mary, Queen of Scots, including her death mask.

*Haddington's Waterside Bistro is a popular spot for a summer lunch*

## JEDBURGH ✪✪✪

This lovely little town with its old wynds (alleys) and houses was established as a Royal Burgh in the 12th century. The immense, graceful ruin of Jedburgh Abbey, founded in 1138, gives the most complete impression of all the Border abbeys' great monastic institutions. It has a haunting abandoned feel to it, as if its medieval inhabitants might return next week to repair the roof. The mellow 16th-century tower house, known as Mary Queen of Scots' House, is worth a visit, too. It wasn't actually her house but she did stay here.

## KELSO ✪

The small market town of Kelso has an enormous cobbled square with a cluster of Georgian houses around it and a maze of cobbled streets leading off. Kelso Abbey suffered badly during the 'Rough Wooing' (➤ 10), and not much remains. Floors Castle, a mile away along the Cobby Riverside walk, is a huge early 18th-century mansion designed by William Adam and still home to the Duke of Roxburgh.

**Mellerstain House**, a few miles distant, is possibly the finest Georgian mansion in Scotland, retaining the original Adam colours in its interior paintwork. Allow half a day to take in the superb collection of paintings, period furniture and terraced gardens.

## MELROSE ✪

Nestling in the Eildon Hills, Melrose is yet another picturesque old abbey town. The heart of Robert the Bruce, who rebuilt the abbey, is buried here. Close by is a Roman three-hill fort, at Newstead, and the **Trimontium Exhibition** in Market Square tells that story.

---

✚ 55E3
✉ 16km (10 miles) southwest of Kelso
☎ 01835 863925
🕐 Apr–Sep, daily 9:30–6:30; Oct–Mar, Mon–Sat 9:30–4:30, Sun 2–4:30
🍴 Cafés and restaurants (£) near by in town
♿ Cheap
❓ Opening times also apply to Dryburgh and Melrose abbeys

✚ 55E3

**Mellerstain House**
✉ Gordon
☎ 01573 410225
🕐 Easter, 1 May–3 Oct, Sun–Fri 12:30–5
🍴 Restaurant (££)
♿ Moderate

Above: *the majestic ruin of Jedburgh Abbey towers over the River Jed*

✚ 55E3

**Trimontium Exhibition**
✉ Ormiston Institute, Market Square
☎ 01896 822651
🕐 Apr–Oct, daily 10:30–4:30
🍴 Cafés and restaurants (£) near by
♿ Cheap

---

> ### DID YOU KNOW?
>
> The word 'dunce' originated from the medieval academic John Duns Scotus who came from the Borders town of Duns. He taught in Oxford and Paris, but when his ideas went out of fashion anyone espousing them became known as a Duns

✚ 55D3
✉ High Street, Innerleithen
☎ 01896 830206
⏰ Good Fri–Easter Mon and May–3 Oct, Mon–Sat 10–1, 2–5, Sun 2–5. Oct weekends same times
🍴 Cafés and restaurants (£) near by
✋ Cheap

✚ 55F4
🍴 Café (£) near harbour

*At St Abbs Head the rolling hills of the Borders give way to rugged cliffs and the North Sea*

## ROBERT SMAILS PRINTING WORKS

The pretty village of Innerleithen is where Robert Smail operated his High Street printing shop in the 19th century. Now in the care of the National Trust for Scotland, it is perfectly preserved. With its Victorian office, composing room, paper store and machine room, there are lots of working exhibits, some hands-on, which can produce authentic Victorian posters and handbills.

## ROSSLYN CHAPEL (➤ 23, TOP TEN)

## ST ABBS ✪✪✪

St Abbs is a working fishing village. You can take a boat trip to get a closer look at the guillemots, kittiwakes, fulmars and razorbills which sweep and squeal and nest around the surrounding rocks and cliffs. Diving, to view the spectacular underwater scenery and sea life in these clear waters, is also possible. The nature reserve, close to the village, offers rock-pool rambles and armchair dives, or you can follow the footpath to the lighthouse to appreciate the wonderful coastline and bird life.

## TRAQUAIR HOUSE (➤ 26, TOP TEN)

# Edinburgh & Borders Drive

*From Princes Street head east along Waterloo Place and Regent Road, then turn right into London Road (A1). Follow it until you see signs for Haddington (▶ 40). Turn right and when your visit is completed, return to the A1 and follow the signs for Berwick-upon-Tweed. After 32km (20 miles), turn left on to the A1107 for Eyemouth, then at Coldingham take a left on to the B6438 to St Abbs (▶ 42). Return via the B6438 to the A1, then turn left and continue until the turn-off for Duns on the A6105.*

**Distance**
265km (165 miles)

**Time**
6–8 hours, depending on stops

**Start/end point**
Edinburgh
✚ 55D4

**Lunch**
Tontine Hotel, High Street, Peebles (after Innerleithen)

Chirnside, which you will pass, was the home of local farmer Jim Clark (1936–68) who was the world motor racing champion twice in the 1960s. Duns, the next town, has a museum dedicated to his life (44 Newtown Street).

*From Duns follow the A6105 to its junction with the A68, turn left and then in a short distance right on to the A6091 until Galashiels, where you turn left on to the A72.*

At Innerleithen you will find Robert Smails Printing Works (▶ 42), and near by is Traquair House (▶ 26).

*Continue on the A72 until it joins the A702 just beyond Skirling. Turn left for Biggar.*

*St Abbs Head is a paradise for bird-watchers and naturalists*

In Biggar is the last gas works in Scotland, preserved as a museum; Gladstone Court, an indoor museum of old shops; and the Biggar Puppet Theatre (▶ 111).

*Leave Biggar (A702) heading back the way you came, signed Edinburgh. After 29km (18 miles), turn right on to the A766 for Penicuick.*

Here you will find the Edinburgh Crystal Visitors' Centre.

*Take the A701 from Penicuik, follow the signs for Roslin village and Rosslyn Chapel (▶ 23), then return to the A701 and follow the signs back to Edinburgh.*

# Glasgow & the Southwest

Glasgow is a fine Victorian city, built on the fortunes of the British Empire. Edinburgh may be the capital of Scotland but Glasgow is its soul. The inhabitants are compulsively outgoing and gregarious so this is not a city to visit if you want to be alone. Sit on a park bench in George Square and within minutes someone will engage you in conversation.

In this area you will find the industrial heart of Scotland, the shipyards of the Clyde, fast-moving computer production, sleepy rural backwaters, the wildernesses of Galloway and miles of coastline. It is a microcosm of Scottish industry, history and literature. Two popular poets, penicillin, tarmacadam, the mackintosh, the bicycle and the pneumatic tyre, not to mention Robert the Bruce and William Wallace, all emerged from the southwest of Scotland.

> *'O beautiful city of Glasgow I must conclude my lay, by calling thee the greatest city of the present day; For your treatment of me was by no means churlish, Therefore I say, 'let Glasgow flourish.'*

WILLIAM TOPAZ MCGONAGAL

●

*The glass-roofed interior of Glasgow's Argyll Arcade built in 1827*

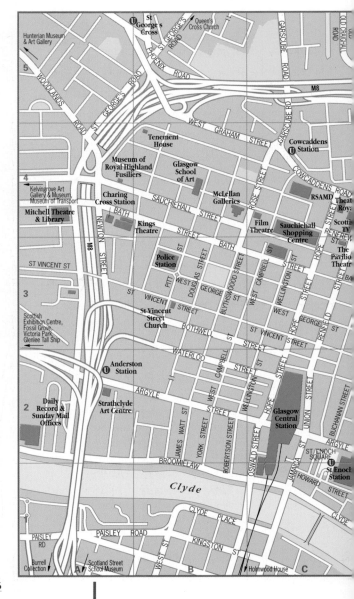

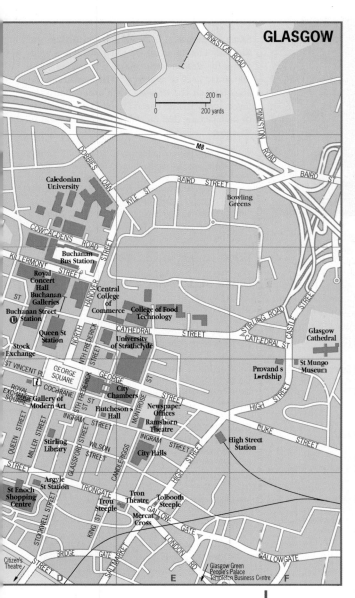

**GLASGOW**

PINKSTON ROAD

PINKSTON ROAD

BAIRD STREET

BAIRD ST

0    200 m
0    200 yards

M8

DOBBIES LOAN

KYLE ST

Caledonian University

Bowling Greens

COWCADDENS ROAD

KILLERMONT ST

Buchanan Bus Station

HANOVER STREET

Royal Concert Hall

Buchanan Galleries

Central College of Commerce

College of Food Technology

STIRLING ROAD

CASTLE STREET

Glasgow Cathedral

Buchanan Street Station

NORTH FREDERICK

CATHEDRAL STREET

CATHEDRAL ST

Queen St Station

University of Strathclyde

Stock Exchange

NTH FREDERICK

St Mungo Museum

ST VINCENT PL

GEORGE SQUARE

GEORGE STREET

Provand's Lordship

ROYAL EXCHANGE SQUARE

COCHRANE ST

STH FREDERICK ST

City Chambers

MONTROSE ST

HIGH STREET

Gallery of Modern Art

INGRAM STREET

Hutcheson's Hall

Newspaper Offices

DUKE STREET

QUEEN STREET

MILLER STREET

GLASSFORD STREET

WILSON STREET

Ramshorn Theatre

Stirling Library

INGRAM STREET

High Street Station

CANDLERIGGS

City Halls

HIGH STREET

Argyle St Station

TRONGATE

St Enoch Shopping Centre

STOCKWELL STREET

KING ST

Tron Theatre

Tron Steeple

Tolbooth Steeple

Mercat Cross

GALLOWGATE

LONDON RD

GALLOWGATE

Citizen's Theatre

BRIDGE GATE

SALTMARKET

Glasgow Green
People's Palace
Templeton Business Centre

D      E      F

Above: *students at Glasgow School of Art*
Right: *Kelvingrove Art Gallery and Museum*

# Glasgow

**Since its portrayal in Alexander MacArthur and Kingsley Long's novel *No Mean City* as a wild, gangster-dominated place, Glasgow has reinvented itself several times. The Garden Festival transformed the derelict dock areas along the Clyde, while The European City of Culture and City of Architecture 1999 proclaimed the stylishness of Glasgow.**

World renowned architects such as Charles Rennie Mackintosh and Alexander 'Greek' Thomson produced what has become one of Europe's best preserved Victorian cities. Imaginative modern designs, including the Burrell Collection and the Armadillo, maintain the standard while 1960s and 1970s architectural blight gradually disappears.

## What to See in Glasgow

**BURRELL COLLECTION (➤ 17, TOP TEN)** FREE

**GALLERY OF MODERN ART** ✪✪

This popular and witty gallery has undermined even the worthy statue of Wellington which fronts it. The great man and his horse are constantly adorned with traffic cones for headgear. In the entrance, the irreverent tone is set by the brilliant, papier mâché caricature of the Queen as a Glasgow housewife, in dressing gown and slippers, with dangling cigarette and copy of *Sporting Life*. The city's collection of art by living artists is housed on four floors.

- 47D2
- Queen Street
- 0141 229 1996
- Mon–Thu and Sat 10–5, Fri and Sun from 11
- Excellent café (£) on premises
- Free

**GLASGOW SCHOOL OF ART** ✪✪✪

Charles Rennie Mackintosh won the competition to design the new school in 1896. It is the earliest example in the UK of a complete art nouveau building, including all the interior furnishings and fittings. Students today still remove books from Mackintosh bookcases and sit on priceless Mackintosh chairs to study them.

- 46B4
- 167 Renfrew Street
- 0141 353 4526
- Guided tours Mon–Fri 11, 2, Sat 10:30, 11:30; additional tours Jul, Aug
- Mackintosh's Willow Tea Room (£) is near by at 217 Sauchiehall Street
- Moderate

> ### DID YOU KNOW?
> The Glasgow Underground, dubbed the Clockwork Orange because of the colour of the trains, is still the best way to get around the city.

## HOLMWOOD HOUSE ⭐⭐

Recently restored by the National Trust for Scotland, Holmwood House, designed by Alexander 'Greek' Thomson, is one of Scotland's finest private villas. The paper magnate James Couper gave Thomson a free hand and he devised an astonishing asymmetrical design. One side has a flat classical frontage with pillars framing the dining-room windows while the bay window on the other side is essentially a circular Greek temple, complete with free-standing pillars, fronting a timber and glass wall. None of the furniture remains but underneath the layers of paper, a remarkable amount of the original paint scheme has survived, including painted scenes of the Trojan Wars.

✚ 46C1
✉ 61 Netherlee Road, Cathcart
☎ 0141 637 2129
🕐 Daily 1:30–5:30 (call to arrange visit)
💷 Cheap
🚌 44, 46
🚆 Glasgow Central (Neilston train to Cathcart station)

## KELVINGROVE ART GALLERY AND MUSEUM ⭐⭐⭐

This elaborately turreted mansion, built of red Dumfriesshire sandstone on the banks of the River Kelvin, is the top free attraction in Scotland. Its art collection includes works by Botticelli, the Pre-Raphaelites, the Impressionists and David Hockney, as well as many great Scottish artists, such as the Glasgow Boys (➤ 57). The museum has collections ranging from Egyptology and prehistory to ship-building and natural history.

✚ 46A4
✉ Argyll Street
☎ 0141 287 2699
🕐 Mon–Thu and Sat 10–5, Fri and Sun from 11
🍴 Tea room on premises (£)
💷 Free
🔁 Museum of Transport (➤ below)

## MUSEUM OF TRANSPORT ⭐⭐⭐

Glasgow's transport museum displays the entire history of Scottish transport, including the pioneer days of the Scottish motor industry. Cars include early Arrol Johnstones produced in Dumfries and the Hillman Imp, built at the long-closed Chrysler plant at Linwood. There is also a whole series of trams, the famous 'Shooglies', the earlier ones resplendent in gleaming brass and polished wood, as well as an entire 1938 street scene with a working cinema and a Victorian underground station.

✚ 46A4
✉ Argyll Street
☎ 0141 287 2700
🕐 Mon–Sat 10–5, Sun from 11
💷 Free
🔁 Kelvingrove Art Gallery and Museum (➤ above)

*Modern-day students get a taste of Victorian education at Scotland Street School Museum*

🕂 46A1
✉ 225 Scotland Street
☎ 0141 287 0500
🕐 Mon–Thu and Sat 10–5, Fri and Sun 2–5
🍴 Good café on premises (£)
♿ Free

### SCOTLAND STREET SCHOOL MUSEUM ●●●
Designed by Charles Rennie Mackintosh, this is an architectural gem, featuring two massive glass-fronted towers. Inside it re-creates the school experience of Scots children from Victorian times through to the 1950s. Classrooms have been reconstructed for several of the periods and in term time visitors in the viewing galleries can watch local children and their teachers dress up in period costume and experience first-hand what it was like. Modern-day kids sometimes feel a little strange as their familiar, friendly teacher is transformed into the fire-breathing dragon of the Victorian classroom. At play time the youngsters take part in games from yesteryear. There are wooden spinning tops, jauries (an old type of marble) and girds and cleeks (hoops and sticks). The only problem for the children is capturing the toys from the grown-ups.

🕂 46A3
✉ Yorkhill Quay, 100 Stobcross Road
☎ 0141 204 4400
🕐 Daily 10–dusk
🍴 Café (£)
♿ Moderate

### THE TALL SHIP AT GLASGOW HARBOUR ●●●
The River Clyde dominated world ship-building well into the 20th century. Many of the legendary liners, the *Queen Mary*, *Queen Elizabeth* and the *QE2*, were built here as well as other less famous ships. The *Glenlee* (1896) is one of the last of the Clyde-built sailing ships and one of only six still afloat. It was in the service of the Spanish navy until the 1970s. Acquired by the Clyde Maritime Trust, who have spent years restoring it, this steel-hulled cargo ship is one of Glasgow's newest attractions.

### THE TENEMENT HOUSE, GLASGOW (► 25, TOP TEN)

# Glasgow Walk

This walk around the centre of the city takes in some interesting buildings and architecture.

*From the tourist office in George Square turn right then right into Miller Street, left along Ingram Street and right into Glassford Street.*

The Tobacco Lairds House is in Miller Street. Glasgow's oldest secular building is the Trades Hall in Glassford Street, designed by Robert Adam in 1794.

*Turn left into Wilson Street, right at Candleriggs and left along the Trongate. Turn right on to Saltmarket and left into Glasgow Green. Follow the paths to the People's Palace and beyond that to Templeton Business Centre.*

Modelled on the Palazzo Ducale in Venice, the multi-coloured, richly patterned Templeton Business Centre was originally a Victorian carpet factory.

*Return to the gates of Glasgow Green and go along Clyde Street. Turn right into Jamaica Street, right into Howard Street and left into St Enoch Square. Across Argyle Street head along Buchanan Street. Walk around Royal Exchange Square on the right. Continue on Buchanan Street then left along St Vincent Street.*

In St Enoch Square the former underground station resembles a miniature château. St Vincent Street Church is the only surviving church of the Victorian architect Alexander 'Greek' Thomson.

*Turn right up Pitt Street and right into Renfrew Street, right at Dalhousie Street and left along Sauchiehall Street.*

In Sauchiehall Street is another Thomson design, the former Grecian Chambers, and the Willow Tea Rooms, owned by Kate Cranston.

*At Buchanan Street turn right, then left along West George Street to return to George Square.*

**Distance**
5–6km (3–4 miles)

**Time**
4 hours

**Start/end point**
George Square
✠ 47D2

**Lunch**
78 St Vincent Street
☎ 0141 248 7878

*The Willow, Glasgow, last remnant of Kate Cranston's famous tea-room, designed by Mackintosh at the end of the 19th century*

51

## What to See in the Southwest

### ARRAN

Reached by Calmac Ferry from Gourock, the island of Arran is a delight. The main town of Brodick with its castle and gardens can be explored in a day-trip. But a few days are necessary to visit the standing stones on Machrie Moor, climb Goatfell or watch the sunset over Ailsa Craig from the south coast. Pottery, paintings, textiles, basketwork and glass, as well as cheese and whisky, are produced locally.

### BURNS NATIONAL HERITAGE PARK (➤ 16, TOP TEN)

**54A4**
Excellent cafés in Brodick (£)
Caledonian MacBrayne Ferry from Gourock

*The triangular design of 13th-century Caerlaverock Castle is unique*

**55D2**
Near Bankend on B725 19km (12 miles) south of Dumfries
01387 770200
Daily 10–5
371 from Dumfries
Cheap

### CAERLAVEROCK CASTLE AND WILDFOWL AND WETLANDS TRUST RESERVE

Thirteenth-century Caerlaverock Castle, dramatically sited on the estuary of the River Nith, is the only triangular castle in Scotland. Built of red sandstone, with an imposing double towered gatehouse, it was protected by a moat and huge ramparts. The castle was besieged, damaged and rebuilt by Scottish and English alike, and changed hands many times over the centuries, particularly during the Wars of Independence (1296–1328). Inside there are the remains of a fine Renaissance mansion house built around 1620. It was finally left a ruin by the depredations of the Covenanters (Scots Protestants) a few years later. Further along the Solway is the Wildfowl and Wetlands Trust Reserve where acres of Merseland (mud flats and salt marshes) are conserved to protect the wildlife and to allow visitors to observe from hides without disturbing the environment. Caerlaverock is home to the most northerly colony of natterjack toads, and every summer the entire Spitsbergen colony of barnacle geese arrives. There are plenty of activities for people of all ages, from bat-watching evenings to pond dipping.

## CULZEAN CASTLE AND COUNTRY PARK ✪✪✪

Perched on a cliff top over the Firth of Clyde, Culzean was constructed for the 10th Earl of Cassillis by the architect Robert Adam. It took 20 years to complete and was finally finished in 1792. Built in neo-Gothic style, with towers and turrets on the outside, the classical design of the inside is dominated by the majestic oval staircase. During his lifetime, the former US President Dwight D Eisenhower had the use of the top floor, and his life and work are commemorated in a permanent display. The castle is set in an extensive country park with gardens, sea-shore, wooded walks and a pond where elegant swans are reflected in its glassy green.

✚ 54B3
✉ 19km (12 miles) southwest of Ayr on A719
☎ (1655 760269
🕐 Apr–Oct 10:30–5. Park: daily 9–sunset
🍴 Tea room in park (££)
♿ Moderate

*Culzean Castle gardens, part of Scotland's first country park*

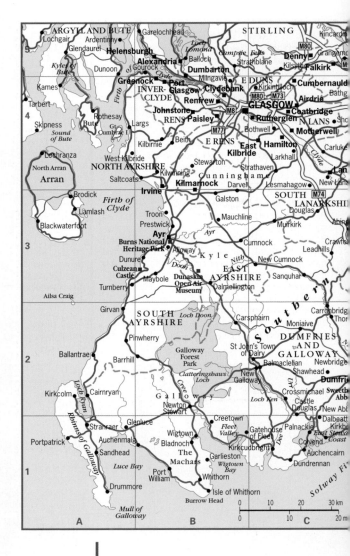

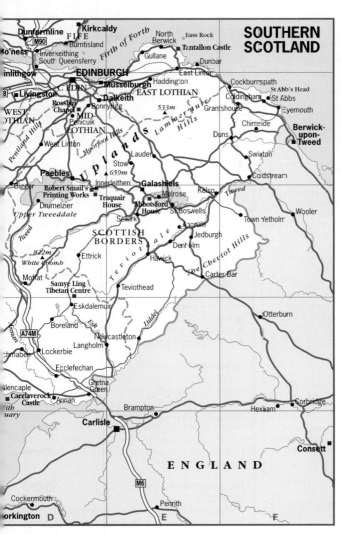

**SOUTHERN SCOTLAND**

Dunfermline
Kirkcaldy
FIFE
Burntisland
M90
'o'ness
Inverkeithing
South Queensferry
Firth of Forth
North Berwick
Bass Rock
Tantallon Castle
inlithgow
Gullane
Dunbar
EDINBURGH
East Linton
Cockburnspath
St Abb's Head
8
Livingston
Musselburgh
Haddington
Coldingham
St Abbs
WEST OTHIAN
C EDIN
Dalkeith
EAST LOTHIAN
Grantshouse
Eyemouth
Rosslyn Chapel
Bonnyrigg
533m
Chirnside
Berwick-upon-Tweed
MID-LOTHIAN
Penicuik
Lauder
Duns
Swinton
Pentland Hills
West Linton
Moorfoot Hills
Lammermuir Hills
Peebles
Uplands
Stow
659m
Coldstream
Bigger
Innerleithen
Galashiels
Tweed
Robert Smail's Printing Works
Traquair House
Melrose
Kelso
Wooler
Abbotsford House
Upper Tweeddale
Selkirk
St Boswells
Tweed
Ancrum
Town Yetholm
SCOTTISH BORDERS
Jedburgh
822m
Ettrick
Teviotdale
Denholm
White Coomb
Hawick
The Cheviot Hills
Moffat
Carter Bar
Samye Ling Tibetan Centre
Teviothead
Otterburn
Eskdalemuir
A74M
Boreland
Esk
Liddel
chmaben
Langholm
Newcastleton
Lockerbie
Ecclefechan
Corbridge
lencaple
Gretna Green
Hexham
Caerlaverock Castle
Annan
Brampton
ith uary
Carlisle
Consett
ENGLAND
M6
Cockermouth
Penrith
orkington
D
E
F

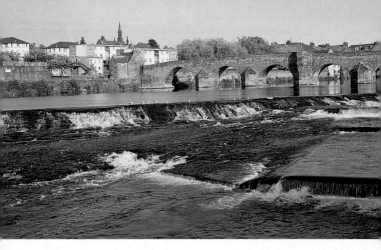

Above: *Devorgilla's
Bridge over the River Nith
at Dumfries*

### DUMFRIES ✪✪

This quiet county town was home to two of Scotland's literary greats, Robert Burns and J M Barrie. Robert Burns, after an unsuccessful farming venture at nearby Ellisland, moved to Dumfries and worked as an Excise man until his untimely death. His house is now a **museum** and on display are the bed he died in and the desk where he copied the words of *Auld Lang Syne*. In the Globe Inn, visitors can sit in the poet's chair but must recite a verse of his poetry or buy the assembled company a drink.

J M Barrie finished his schooling at Dumfries Academy, and it was while playing pirates with his friends in a garden next to the school that Peter Pan was born. The garden was the inspiration for Never Never Land and Captain Hook was his maths master. In Dumfries Museum the earliest example of Barrie's writing can be seen.

### DUNASKIN OPEN AIR MUSEUM ✪✪✪

This is the best preserved Victorian ironworks in Europe. Sited in the countryside, close to the Ayrshire coal fields, it survived because there was no need to demolish it for the space. There are delightful walks through Dunaskin Glen, a period cottage and an opportunity to experience working in a coal mine. An audio-visual re-creates Ayrshire life in the 19th and early 20th centuries and there are lots of hands-on activities for children.

### GALLOWAY FOREST PARK AND ✪✪✪
### GLENTROOL

The Galloway Forest Park centred around lovely Loch Trool and the Galloway Hills is an area of outstanding natural beauty. Hill-walking in this empty wilderness is rewarded by splendid views over lochs, hills and coast. Less strenuous is a stroll or cycle through the myriad forest paths or a drive along the Queen's Way to the pretty village of New Galloway.

## KIRKCUDBRIGHT ✪✪

There is a magic quality to the light in this part of the world that draws artists to set up home. The illustrator Jessie M King and her husband, E A Taylor, lived at Green Gate Close in High Street, while Edward Hornel, one of the Glasgow Boys, a group of Scottish painters who were inspired by the Impressionists, lived near by at **Broughton House**. Hornel's Georgian mansion, with its delightful Japanese garden, is now a museum to his life and work. In the Old Tolbooth is an art centre featuring the work of local artists. Also worth a visit is the Stewartry Museum and MacLellan's Castle, which dominates the square beside the picturesque but still working harbour.

🔲 54C1

**Broughton House**
✉ High Street
☎ 01557 330437
🕐 Apr–Oct, daily 1–5:30
🍴 Tea room near by (£)
♿ Cheap

*St Ninian's Priory Church, Whithorn, near the first Christian settlement in Scotland*

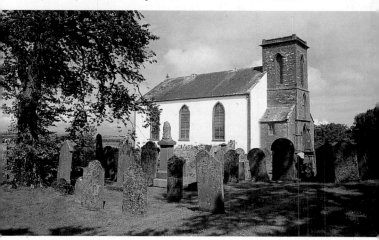

## THE MACHARS ✪✪

This peninsula south of Newton Stewart is a time warp, reminiscent of the Sunday afternoons of yesteryears. Wigtown, once a prosperous and bustling county town, looks and feels like a ghost town, but poke about in the new book shops opening up all over the place and underneath the surface it is evident that a new prosperity is emerging.

Further south is the sleepy town of Whithorn, where Christianity first came to Scotland with St Ninian in AD 397. Pilgrims flocked here from all over the Christian world until pilgrimage was banned during the Reformation. Much of medieval Whithorn remains, and at the **Whithorn Dig** the earlier settlements are being excavated.

🔲 54B1

**Whithorn Dig**
✉ George Street
☎ 01988 500508
🕐 Apr–Oct, daily 10:30–5
🍴 Tea room near by (£)
♿ Cheap

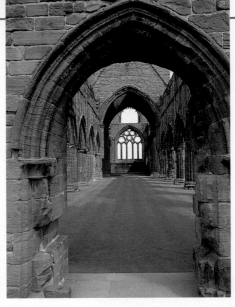

*Sweetheart Abbey, last resting place of the hearts of Devorgilla de Balliol and her husband*

➕ 54C2

**Sweetheart Abbey**
⊠ New Abbey
☎ 01387 850397
⊘ Apr–Sep, daily 9:30–6:30;
   Oct–Mar, Mon–Wed and
   Sat 9:30–4.30, Thu
   9:30–12:30, Sun 2–4:30
🍴 The excellent New Abbey
   Tea Room is adjacent (£)
💷 Cheap
🚌 372 from Dumfries

➕ 55D3
⊠ Eskdalemuir
☎ 01387 373232
⊘ Daily
🍴 Café on site (£)
💷 Free
🚌 112 from Langholm

### NEW ABBEY ✪✪

Nestling under the shadow of Criffel, the village of New Abbey is dominated by the ruins of a Cistercian abbey. It was founded in 1273 by Devorgilla de Balliol, wife of the Scottish king John Balliol, founder of Balliol College, Oxford and became known as **Sweetheart Abbey** because the hearts of Devorgilla and her husband are interred together here.

New Abbey Cornmill is a water-driven mill in the care of the National Trust for Scotland, with working machinery. Close to New Abbey is the museum of costume and dress at Shambellie House, and at Arbigland, near the village of Kirkbean, is the cottage birthplace of John Paul Jones (1747–92), founder of the United States Navy.

If the sky is clear a climb to Criffel's peak, 570m, will provide a view into four kingdoms – Scotland, Ireland, England and the Isle of Man.

### NEW LANARK (► 22, TOP TEN)

### SAMYE LING TIBETAN CENTRE ✪✪

Probably the last thing you would expect to find in this remote and lonely corner of Dumfries and Galloway is a Buddhist monastery. Yet here it is in all its splendour. Elaborate oriental buildings in bright red and gold sit high up in the Southern Uplands of Scotland with the tranquil sounds of wind chimes filling the air. Tibetan monks built Samye Ling, but it is home to a community of Buddhists. There are various courses in meditation on offer, including weekend workshops and retreats, and visitors are very welcome.

# The Southwest Drive

This drive will take you through some of the finest scenery in Scotland – rugged mountains, rocky coastline, low-lying pastures and picturesque towns and villages.

*From Dumfries follow the A710 via New Abbey, Kirkbean and Colvend to Dalbeattie.*

The John Paul Jones birthplace museum near Kirkbean (► 58) is a tribute to the Scot who founded the American Navy. New Abbey is the site of Sweetheart Abbey (► 58).

*From Dalbeattie take the A711 to Kirkcudbright, then the A762 to New Galloway.*

Tiny Palnackie is the venue for the annual World Flounder Tramping Championships. Here competitors stand in the water, waiting until they feel a flounder moving under their feet, then reach down and scoop the fish up. At Dundrennan is another ruined abbey.

*From New Galloway turn right on to the A712 to Balmaclellan, then the B7075 and right on to the A702 to Moniaive.*

The clogmaker at Balmaclellan welcomes visitors to his workshop, while the picturesque village of Moniaive has the James Patterson Museum, devoted to the work of one of the Glasgow Boys who lived there.

*Take the B729 just beyond Kirkland to Dunscore, then turn right on to a local road heading towards Newtonairds and follow the signs for Shawhead.*

At Glenkiln Reservoir, a collection of sculptures by Henry Moore, Jacob Epstein and Auguste Rodin is displayed in the sweeping pastoral landscape. Moore's King and Queen sculpture on the hillside overlooking the reservoir has become the symbol of Glenkiln.

*From Glenkiln continue along the side of the reservoir to Shawhead; follow the local road to the A75, turn left and return to Dumfries.*

**Distance**
153km (95 miles)

**Time**
6–8 hours depending on stops

**Start/end point**
Dumfries
✚ 54C2

**Lunch**
Craigdarroch Arms, Moniaive (£)

*Ancient carvings in the ruins of Dundrennan Abbey*

# Food & Drink

Traditional Scottish cooking can be a culinary delight, but perseverance is required to find good examples. The poor diet of many Scots has dubbed Scotland the heart attack capital of Europe. Avoid the deep-fried Mars bar, but a fish supper (fish in batter with chips) can be good, especially in fishing areas.

*Smoked Scottish salmon – just add lemon juice*

**Food for a Parliament**
Kinfauns Castle (► 97) in Perthshire, the magnificent setting of regular Gourmet Evenings, is one of the best places in Scotland to enjoy fresh Scottish produce, cooked with traditional skills and continental flare. Its head chef, Jeremy Wares, Restaurant Chef of the Year 1999, was one of the top chefs chosen to cook a gourmet Scottish dinner for the opening of the Scottish Parliament in 1999.

## Fish

As a fishing nation, the traditional food of the poor was tatties and herring (boiled potatoes with herring in oatmeal). The Arbroath smokie, whole haddock smoked in the traditional way, is the gourmet smoked fish, delicious cooked with milk and butter. Avoid the vivid deep-dyed yellow of the chemically processed smoked haddock. Cullen skink, a soup made from smoked haddock, potatoes, onions and cream, is practically a meal in itself. Salmon is readily available since the increase in fish farming, but wild salmon can be found at good fishmongers. It may cost more but the taste is superb.

## Meat

Haggis is the best-known Scottish meat dish, made from sheep offal, blood, spices and oatmeal and boiled in a sheep's stomach. If that makes you squeamish you can get a vegetarian version, made from nuts and pulses.

Traditionally it is eaten with mashed tatties (potatoes) and neeps (turnips) but Stac Polly restaurants in Edinburgh serve haggis in filo pastry with plum sauce. The traditional dish to serve at New Year is steak pie. Good butchers make their own steak pies, which have flaky pastry and a rich gravy, and mutton pies with thin, dry pastry filled with minced meat.

## Oat Cuisine and Dining Out

A traditional Scottish breakfast starts with porridge, (▶ panel) followed by eggs, bacon, square slice (a kind of beef sausage), black pudding (a spicy blood pudding), potato scones and tomatoes. This comes with copious quantities of tea, buttered rolls and marmalade. If you need lunch after this, pick up a midday snack of Scotch Broth or pie and beans in a pub or café.

For eating out in the evening, there are many excellent restaurants specialising in traditional and imaginative Scottish menus. A typical menu might start with smoked salmon or partan bree (crab soup), serve high-quality Aberdeen Angus or game as a main course and finish off with the luxurious cranachan, a dish which combines toasted oatmeal with raspberries, cream, honey and whisky. Before or after the pudding, local cheeses such as Dunsyre Blue or Dunlop might be served with oatcakes. Traditionally, fine food is accompanied by French wine but to round off the evening try Drambuie, a whisky-based liqueur made from a secret recipe originating with Bonnie Prince Charlie.

## The National Drink

Whisky, Scotland's national drink is distilled from barley. There are hundreds of malt whiskies, aged for 10 or 12 years, sometimes more in wooden casks. The flavour of each malt reflects the spring water, the peat, the type of cask and the years of maturation. Most pubs have a selection of the better-known malts.

Advertised as 'Scotland's other national drink', Irn-Bru is a sickly orange-coloured fizzy drink, reputed to cure hangovers. There could be no other reason for drinking it.

**Oats**
Oatmeal is a staple Scottish ingredient. Porridge, made by cooking oatmeal in water or milk, is eaten salted, sometimes with cream, never with sugar. In times past, cooked porridge would be poured into the bottom drawer of a dresser, then cut into slices and eaten cold. Oatcakes are made from oatmeal flour and butter. The mass-produced version tastes like cardboard, but there are dozens of small local producers making delicious variations.

*Haggis, 'Great chieftain o' the Puddin' race!'*

# Central Scotland

This disparate cross-section of Scotland stretches from the lonely island-scattered western coastline of Argyll and the Hebrides to the fishing villages of the East Neuk of Fife on the Firth of Forth, all the way to the silvery Tay, Angus and the featureless expanse of the North Sea beyond. It includes wild hills, moorlands and waterways, the bustling small towns of Scotland's central belt and lush agricultural land.

Rising in the great central plain is the rocky prominence of Stirling Castle, which saw some of the fiercest fighting in the Scottish Wars of Independence (1296–1328), while further north lie the refined country town of Perth, down-to-earth Dundee and the heather-covered splendour of the Angus Glens.

> *'And far abin the Angus straths I*
> *saw the wild geese flee,*
> *A lang, lang skein o beatin wings*
> *wi their heids toward the sea,*
> *And aye their cryin voices trailed*
> *ahint them on the air.'*
> *'Oh wind, hae mercy, haud your*
> *wheesht for I daurna listen mair.'*

VIOLET JACOB
1915

# Dundee

**Dundee straggles untidily along the River Tay, its two distinctive bridges reaching out long thin highways of road and rail over the broad stretch of water to Fife. Of the three Js – jute, jam and journalism – which were the lifeblood of the town, only journalism remains, in the shape of D C Thomson, who publish the *Dandy* and the *Beano* comics and the *Sunday Post*. In the surrounding countryside, the many berry fields which used to supply the jam factories now allow you to pick your own fruit. The town has reinvented itself as a popular conference centre, assisted by the unassuming**

**friendliness of the people. This, together with the unpretentious cultural life, excellent museums and small theatres, make it an agreeable base for touring the area.**

Captain Scott's ship Discovery, *Dundee's premier tourist attraction*

## What to See in Dundee

### BROUGHTY FERRY AND CASTLE ✪

Broughty Ferry, once a separate village, is now a suburb of Dundee. It is popular with Dundonians and visitors alike, with its eclectic mix of restaurants, pubs and shops and sandy beach along the banks of the silvery Tay. Fifteenth-century **Broughty Castle**, now a museum, tells the story of Broughty Ferry and the whaling industry.

✚ 79E2

**Broughty Castle**
☎ 01382 436916
🕐 Tue–Sat 11–5, Sun 12:30–4; closed Mon Oct–Mar  🎟 Free

### RRS *DISCOVERY* AND ✪✪✪
### HM FRIGATE *UNICORN*

Once the pride of the Panmuir yard, where she was built in 1901 for the polar expeditions of Captain Robert Falcon Scott, the **Royal Research Ship** *Discovery* lay rotting for years on the Thames Embankment in London. Finally returned to her birthplace, restored, and housed at the purpose-built Discovery Point, she is now a major tourist attraction.

The Frigate *Unicorn*, further along the Tay at Victoria Dock, is the oldest British warship still afloat. Built in 1824, she was, incredibly, still in service until 1968.

✚ 79E2

**RRS *Discovery***
✉ Victoria Quay, near the Tay Bridge
☎ 01382 201245
🕐 Apr–Oct, Mon–Sat 10–5, Sun 11–5; Nov–Mar, Mon–Sat 10–4, Sun 11–4
🍴 Café (£)
♿ Very good
👐 Moderate

**79E2**

Albert Square, city centre

01382 432084

Mon–Sat 10–5, (until 7 Thu), Sun 12:30–4

Café (£)

Very good

Free

---

**79E2**

Balgay Park. Approach via Perth Road, Blackness Avenue, Balgay Road

01382 435846

Apr–Sep, Tue–Fri 11–5, Sat, Sun 12:30–4; Oct–Mar, Mon–Fri 4–10, Sat, Sun 12:30–4

Few

Free

Booking essential for large groups and for Planetarium

---

*McManus Art Gallery, Victorian splendour in Dundee*

---

**79E2**

27 West Henderson's Wynd

01382 225282

Apr–Oct 10–5; Nov–Mar 11–4

Refreshments (£)

Very good

Expensive

## MCMANUS ART GALLERY AND MUSEUM

This is an absolute gem of a place, one of the finest Victorian buildings in Dundee, and that's just the outside. Indoors, the museum covers Dundee's history from the ancient Picts to modern times. There's also a great display on the Tay Bridge disaster. On 28 December, 1879, the bridge collapsed in a storm after only 18 months, and 75 people died. Upstairs in the Albert Hall, with its pitch pine-panelled roof, are collections of glass, gold, silver, musical instruments and furniture, including the table where the death warrants for captured Jacobites were signed by the Duke of Cumberland after the Battle of Culloden in 1746. The art collection in the Victoria Gallery includes several Scottish collections and some superb Pre-Raphaelites.

## MILLS OBSERVATORY

This is the only public observatory in Britain, and the enthusiastic and knowledgeable resident astronomer is a delight to talk to. There are special openings for eclipses and the odd visiting comet. Winter evenings are obviously the best time to go, but in the summer months, when it's light, there are exhibits and displays well worth seeing.

## VERDANT WORKS

Verdant Works was one of Dundee's many jute mills which produced hessian and sacking, and once employed 50,000 people locally; it has been restored and reconstructed as a museum. Volunteers operate textile machines, while 'Juteopolis', a 15-minute film, explains the dramatic impact of the industry on the city and its people. Every day at 1PM the works' 'bummer' (factory whistle) is blown, a sound that marked the livelihood of many families in Dundee and recalls its history in an evocative way.

# Central Scotland Drive

*Start from Perth. Take the A85, then turn right on to the A93 and right again on to the A94. (Scone Palace is 2.5km/1½ miles further along the A93.) At Balbeggie, take the B953 to Inchture, then turn left on to the A90. Take the A85 left through Dundee, past Discovery Point and follow the signs for the Tay Bridge and the A92. Pass through Newport-on-Tay and Leuchars to St Andrews, then follow the A917. Follow the coastline of the East Neuk, diverting through the picturesque villages of Crail, Anstruther, Pittenweem, St Monance and Elie.*

From Crail take the B940 to Scotland's Secret Bunker. This underground relic of the Cold War would have become the administrative centre of Scotland in the event of a nuclear attack. It was an official secret until 1994 when it opened to the public. Part of it is still operational.

*Turn left on to the A915.*

Have a look at Lower Largo, with its statue of Alexander Selkirk, the prototype of Robinson Crusoe. A native of Largo, Selkirk ran away to sea and was marooned on Juan Fernand Island from 1705 to 1709.

*Continue on the A91, then turn right on to the A911 and in Glenrothes turn right on to the A92, then left on to the A912. At Falkland follow the B936 to Auchtermuchty and turn left on to the A91. From the A91 turn left on to the B919, left on to the A911, then after Kinnesswood, right on to the B920. At the junction turn right on to the B9097, right again on to the B996 and continue to Kinross.*

This route circles Loch Leven with the 14th-century ruins of Loch Leven Castle on an island. Mary, Queen of Scots, was imprisoned here in 1567.

*Take the A922 to Milnathort and the B996 via Glenfarg to the A912. Turn left and follow the road through Bridge of Earn back to Perth.*

**Distance**
190km (118 miles)

**Time**
6–8 hours including stops

**Start/end point**
Perth
79D1

**Lunch**
The Naafi at the Secret Bunker (£)
☎ 0133 310301

*Maintaining the fishing fleet in Pittenweem*

65

## What to See in Central Scotland

### THE ANGUS GLENS

The Glens of Angus are a series of five glorious glens to the north of Dundee. Rich in wildlife and a botanist's paradise, look out particularly for red deer and arctic plants. Glen Clova is probably the most picturesque, and there are several lovely walks to choose from. Jock's Road, which leads through the mountains to Braemar, some 22.5km (14 miles) away, is spectacular. The path clings, precariously at times, to the edge of the hill, the water runs far below and, as you climb, the view of the glen behind falls away in a changing and winding perspective, misty in the distance. Passable only in summer, don't even think about it between October and March.

🕀 79E2

*Below: Crarae, one of the finest gardens in Scotland*

### BO'NESS AND KINNIEL RAILWAY

This is one of the best of the small independent railway lines, situated in the town of Bo'ness, the largest centre for vintage trains in Scotland. Five kilometres (3 miles) of track leads to Birkhill, where you can visit the Birkhill Clay Mine or stroll in the Avon Gorge before the old steam train departs for the return journey.

🕀 79D1
✉ Off Union Street, Bo'ness
☎ 01506 822298
✋ Apr–Oct, every weekend (Jul–Aug Tue–Sun); Santa Specials Dec weekends
✋ Moderate

### CRARAE GARDEN

Between Inveraray and Lochgilphead, this garden is laid out round the glen of the Crarae Burn which flows into Loch Fyne. Covering over 20ha, there are two walking routes, the inner and outer circles which both start from the car-park. Strategically placed seats allow you to enjoy majestic views over Loch Fyne while admiring the snowdrops, daffodils, bluebells, azaleas, rhododendrons or magnolias according to season.

🕀 78C1
✉ A83, 16km (10 miles) southwest of Inveraray
☎ 01546 886614
✋ Daily 9–6 (dusk in winter)
🍴 Refreshments (£)
✋ Moderate

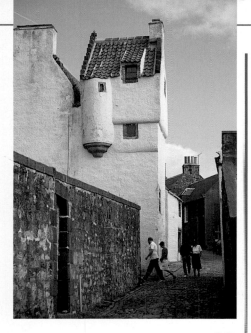

## CULROSS AND CULROSS PALACE ✪✪

The National Trust for Scotland tends the red-tiled houses
and whitewashed walls of this delightful town. Walk
through the cobbled Back Causeway, visit the remains of
the Cistercian Culross Abbey, or the Study, a restored
17th-century house. The 16th-century merchant's house
known as **Culross Palace** is the main attraction, with little
rooms and narrow passages. St Mungo, the founder, and
patron saint of Glasgow, was reputedly born here.

🕂 79D1
✉ 12km (7½ miles) west of
Dunfermline

**Culross Palace**
☎ 01383 880359
🕐 Apr–Sep, daily 11–5
🍴 Café (£)
♿ Moderate

## DOUNE CASTLE ✪

The ruins of Doune's 14th-century castle are the only clue
to the town's turbulent past. The castle, a formidable
range of buildings surrounding an inner courtyard,
belonged to James Stewart, second Earl of Moray and
half-brother of Mary, Queen of Scots. He was murdered in
1592, as told in the ballad 'The Bonnie Earl of Moray'.

🕂 79D1
✉ Off the A84 at Doune
☎ C1786 841742
🕐 Apr–Sep, daily 9:30–6:30;
Oct–Mar, Mon–Wed, Sat
9:30–4:30, Thu 9:30–
12:30, Sun 2–4:30

## EAST NEUK OF FIFE ✪✪✪

The coastline of the East Neuk (neuk is Scots for corner) is
dotted with a string of little fishing villages. Quaint
cottages with red-tiled roofs and crow-stepped gables
perch around secluded harbours. Crail is without a doubt
the prettiest, while Anstruther and Pittenweem are still
regular working ports. Anstruther is home to the **Scottish
Fisheries Museum**, where the entire history of fishing in
Scotland unfolds. Kellie Castle, to the north of Anstruther,
is a 16th-century building, restored during the late 19th
century. It has a splendid garden full of delightful nooks
and crannies, paths and arches.

🕂 79E1

**Scottish Fisheries Museum**
✉ Anstruther Harbour
☎ 01333 310628
🕐 Apr–Oct, Mon–Sat
10–5:30, Sun 11–5;
Nov–Mar, Mon–Sat
10–4:30, Sun 2-4:30
🍴 Tea room (£)
♿ Moderate

78C1

**Hill House**
✉ Upper Colquhoun Street
☎ 01436 673900
🕐 Apr–Dec, daily 1:30–5
🍴 Tea room (£)
♿ Moderate

Opposite: *Inveraray Castle, seat of the Dukes of Argyll*

78B2

*Tobermory harbour with its gaily coloured cottages*

### HELENSBURGH AND HILL HOUSE ✪✪✪

The main attraction in this attractive Georgian town on the Firth of Clyde is **Hill House**, designed by Charles Rennie Mackintosh in 1902 for the publisher Walter Blackie. Mackintosh was given a completely free hand in the design of the house, its interior and furnishings. The result is one of the finest art nouveau houses in Britain, now painstakingly restored by The National Trust for Scotland. The exterior echoes a traditional tower with its irregular windows, round turret and solid expanses of wall. Inside, it is light and elegant with perfect proportions and delightful glimpses of the adjoining spaces as you move through it.

Henry Bell, the inventor of the *Comet*, an early steam-driven boat, was bathing master in Helensburgh, which was also the birthplace of the inventor of television, John Logie Baird.

### THE INNER HEBRIDES ✪✪

There's a magical quality about the islands of Islay, Jura, Mull, Iona, Coll and Tiree. Most tourists head for Tobermory on Mull, with its gaily coloured houses fronting the harbour where, tradition has it, the wreck of a Spanish galleon lies laden with gold. Iona, with its mighty cathedral and connections with St Columba, draws pilgrims from all over the world. Jura has wonderful, blindingly white, sandy beaches that are all but deserted – just the spot to get away from it all. But it is to Islay that you must go if you want to experience some of the finest whiskies in Scotland. Islay malts are unique and easily distinguished by their smokey, peaty taste.

## INVERARAY ✪✪

This small 18th-century town, built by the Duke of Argyll, clan chief of the Campbells, has an enchanting view over Loch Fyne. The old gaol and adjoining court-house are now a museum. Inveraray Castle, home of the Duke of Argyll, would not be out of place on the Loire. In the stable block the Combined Operations Museum is dedicated to the troops that trained on Loch Fyne for the D-Day landings in Normandy. Inside the castle itself is a collection of weapons given to the Campbells by the government to help repress the Jacobites.

Southwest of Inveraray is the restored township of **Auchindrain**, now a folk museum, with around 20 thatched cottages set up to re-create life prior to the Clearances.

✚ 78C1

**Auchindrain**
- ✉ 8km (5 miles) southwest of Inveraray
- ☎ 01499 500235
- 🕐 Apr–Jun and Sep–early Oct, Mon–Thu and Sat 10–noon, 2–5, Sun 1–5; Jul–Aug, Mon–Sat 10–5, Sun 1–5
- 🍴 Tea room (£)
- ♿ Moderate

## KIRRIEMUIR ✪✪

Kirriemuir was the birthplace of J M Barrie, novelist, dramatist and creator of *Peter Pan*. The house he was born in is now a **museum**, and outside is the wash-house, the prototype of the house the Lost Boys built for Wendy, which the young Barrie used as a theatre for his first plays. Barrie is buried in the local cemetery.

✚ 79E2

**J M Barrie Musuem**
- ✉ 9 Brechin Road
- ☎ 01575 572646
- 🕐 Phone for opening times
- ♿ Cheap

## LINLITHGOW ✪✪

Mary, Queen of Scots, was born here at **Linlithgow Palace** in 1542. Although a royal building had existed here since the time of David I (1124–53), it was James I who built the present one. It survived until 1746 when it was destroyed by fire, but it's well worth a visit. Overlooking Linlithgow Loch, the roofless ruin has spiral staircases, stately rooms, a magnificent Great Hall, and a brewery down below.

✚ 79D1

**Linlithgow Palace**
- ✉ South shore of loch
- ☎ 01506 842896
- 🕐 Apr–Sep, daily 9:30–6:30; Oct–Mar, Mon–Sat 9:30–4:30, Sun 2–4:30
- ♿ Cheap

**78C1**

**Bonawe Iron Furnace**
- Off the A85 at Bonawe
- 01866 822432
- Mar–Sep, daily 9:30–6:30; Oct–Nov Mon–Sat 9:30–4:30, Sun 2–4
- Cheap

**78C1**
- Near the marina in Balloch
- Apr–Oct, daily 10–5 (Jul and Aug 9:30–7:30)

Above: *romantic Loch Awe and Kilchurn Castle, a 15th-century Campbell stronghold*

**79E2**
- 1.5km (1 mile) from Montrose, on the A92
- 01674 676336
- Apr–Oct, daily 10:30–5; Nov–Mar, daily 10:30–4
- Moderate

## LOCH AWE

This is the longest freshwater loch in Scotland. There are forest walks at Barnaline, near Dalavich, and near the head of the loch you will find the tiny island of Inishail, with its 13th-century chapel. At Taynuilt, visit the restored industrial heritage centre of **Bonawe Iron Furnace** before heading back towards the loch via the gloomy Pass of Brander for a tour of the Cruachan Power Station. The station is built into Ben Cruachan, where hydroelectricity is generated by water pumped up the mountain from the loch below.

## LOCH LOMOND

Loch Lomond is terribly overcrowded during the tourist season but it is one of Scotland's great beauty spots. The pretty village of Luss doubles as the fictional Glendarroch in Scottish Television's soap opera *Take the High Road*. To escape the crowds take one of the many boat trips from Balloch which head round the small islands on the loch, or follow the West Highland Way on the east bank to Balmaha and Rowardennan. This is grand walking country and the starting point to climb Ben Lomond, 972m.

## MONTROSE BASIN WILDLIFE CENTRE

The Basin is a huge tidal lagoon of mud that is a rich habitat for all manner of wildlife. Humans may hold their noses but to the geese, waders and swans that frequent the basin, grubbing in the smelly mud is a gourmet experience. Telescopes, binoculars and video cameras are strategically placed to enable visitors to watch without disturbing the birds, and there is a regular series of guided walks led by the resident ranger.

## OBAN ✪

Oban, the main ferry terminal for Caledonian MacBrayne Ferries, is known as the gateway to the Isles. McCaig's Folly, a granite tower, was built for no real reason on a hill overlooking the town, however, it looks dramatic, particularly when floodlit at night. Outside the town are the ruins of 13th-century **Dunstaffanage Castle**, where Flora MacDonald was imprisoned after assisting in the escape of Bonnie Prince Charlie. The Isle of Kerrera in Oban Bay, with a population of less than 50, is easily reached by passenger ferry. It is a peaceful retreat with great views over to Mull and Jura.

✚ 78C1

**Dunstaffnage Castle**

✉ 5km (3 miles) north of Oban, off the A85

☎ 01631 562465

🕐 Apr–Sep, daily 9:30–6:30 (4:30 Oct–Mar)

✋ Cheap

*The magnificent interior of historic Scone Palace*

## PERTH ✪✪

Once the capital of Scotland, Perth is now a prosperous market town in the heart of rich farmlands. Visit the Victorian water-driven oat mill at Lower City Mills and the cobbled streets around it. Bell's Cherrybank Gardens has the largest collection of heathers in Britain and a super children's play area, and at the Caithness Glass factory you can see glass blown in the traditional way.

Scone, a couple of miles north, where all the monarchs of Scotland were crowned on the Stone of Destiny, is the historic heart of Scotland. Ancient **Scone Palace** was restored and extended in the 19th century and this elegant, restrained, Gothic mansion is home to the Earl of Mansfield. The grounds, the house and the history are fascinating, but there is also an extraordinary collection of furniture, porcelain, delicate ivories, and papier mâché which once belonged to Louis XV of France.

✚ 79D1

**Scone Palace**

✉ Off the A93 Braemar Road, 3km (2 miles) northeast of Perth

☎ 01738 552300

🕐 Easter–late Oct, daily 9:30–5:45

🍽 Restaurant (££) and coffee shop (£)

✋ Moderate

79D2

**Pass of Killiecrankie**

✉ Off the A9, 5km (3 miles) north of Pitlochry

☎ 01796 473233

🕐 Visitors' centre: Apr–Oct, daily 10–5:30

🍴 Snack bar (£)

👢 Cheap

79E1

**British Golf Museum**

✉ Bruce Embankment, opposite the Royal and Ancient Golf Club

☎ 01334 478880

🕐 Easter to mid-Oct 9:30–5:30; winter Thu–Mon 11–3

👢 Moderate

*Did this figure once ward off evil spirits at St Andrews Cathedral?*

79D1

**Stirling Castle**

✉ Castle Wynd

☎ 01786 450000

🕐 Apr–Sep, daily 9:30–6; Oct–Mar, daily 9:30–5

🍴 Tea room (£)

👢 Moderate

## PITLOCHRY ✪✪

Pitlochry is a popular tourist centre on the banks of the River Tummel, where the Blair Athol Distillery has been making its famous malt since 1798. The power station produces electricity from the artificially created Loch Faskally, and the salmon ladder to help the fish negotiate the dam is a sight not to be missed. Pitlochry Festival Theatre is famous for its productions. Enjoy a backstage tour during the day and return in the evening for a performance of the latest play.

Near the town is the **Pass of Killiecrankie**, site of the famous Battle of Killicrankie in 1689 where the Jacobites, led by Graham of Claverhouse (Bonnie Dundee), defeated the government forces, although Dundee himself was killed. This deep wooded gorge has a visitors' centre with exhibits on the gorge and the battle.

## ST ANDREWS ✪✪

Scotland's oldest university town is world famous as the home of golf, which has been played here since the 15th century. The Royal and Ancient Golf Club is the governing body of the sport and in 1873 the first British Open Championship was held here. The **British Golf Museum** is the best there is, with lots of hands-on stuff and plenty of history. However, if golf is not your scene take a walk around the historic streets to the great cathedral, once the largest in Scotland. It was consecrated in 1318 in the presence of King Robert the Bruce and destroyed in 1559 by supporters of John Knox. An impressive ruin, it is particularly beautiful at twilight in half silhouette.

## STIRLING ✪✪✪

**Stirling Castle**, like Edinburgh, is perched atop the plug of an extinct volcano, but in many ways Stirling is more dramatic. Surrounded by a wide plain, the castle is the most prominent sight for miles around and in past times the narrow bridge here was a strategic gateway between North and South. Many of the decisive battles in Scotland's history, including Stirling Bridge (1297) and Bannockburn (1314) were fought around here. At the

Lady's Rock in the cemetery there is a pointer to all the surrounding battle sites. Bannockburn's visitors' centre details the battle in an excellent audio-visual presentation. The Wallace Monument high on the cliffs overlooking the site of the Battle of Stirling Bridge contains the hero's massive two-handed sword.

### THE TROSSACHS ✪✪✪

This wild countryside of moors, hills and forests, from Loch Katrine to Loch Lomond, was the haunt of Rob Roy MacGregor – outlaw, cattle thief, murderer or Scottish hero depending on your point of view. At any rate he died at a ripe old age in his own bed and is buried in the beautiful churchyard at Balquhidder. The Trossachs is the largest area of wilderness in central Scotland. There is excellent walking, climbing and fishing and the scenery is spectacular. If you can't make it to the Highlands, this is as near as you'll get to the majestic scale of the north. Its position right at the heart of Scotland means that it is easily accessible, but unfortunately, always crowded.

The two main towns in the area are Callander and Aberfoyle.

✝ 79D1

ℹ Stirling and Trossachs Tourist Board Old Town Jail, St John's Street, Stirling ☎ 01786 445222; fax: 01786 471301

*Loch Katrine in the heart of MacGregor country*

# The North

The Highlands and Islands are the Scotland of literature, romance and the movies, a vast area, much of it unforgiving mountain or natural moorland. Many species of wildlife which have disappeared elsewhere survive in the scarcely populated wildernesses here. Scattered ruined cottages remain, testimony to a more populous past before the Clearances in the 18th and 19th centuries, when the landlords drove the people from the land in favour of more profitable sheep.

Highlanders emigrated in droves to the New World, taking with them their oral traditions of music and storytelling and their memories of the land they left behind. Exiled Scots and their descendants get very nostalgic at the mention of misty glens, heather-covered hillsides and dark deep lochs. It is easy to mock, but travel this land once and you will understand how they feel.

> *'From the long shieling of the misty island, mountains divide us and a waste of seas. Yet still the blood is strong, the heart is Highland, and we in dreams behold The Hebrides.'*

ANON

# Aberdeen

Aberdeen, the grey granite city of the North, is the hub of Scotland's oil industry, a thriving fishing port and home to one of the four ancient universities of Scotland. Surprisingly, for the most northerly city of Scotland, it is famed for its imaginative and prolific gardens. The nightlife is lively on account of the university and the prosperity of its cosmopolitan population. Understanding the language, however, can present problems and a crash course in the Doric, the local dialect, might be a good idea. In the meantime, to the standard greeting of 'Fit like?', simply answer 'Nae bad, foo's yersel?' Translated it means 'How are you ?', 'Not bad, how are you?'

## What to See in Aberdeen

### ABERDEEN MARITIME MUSEUM ⭐⭐

The 1953 Provost Ross's house, one of the oldest buildings in the city, is home to this remarkable museum which tells the story of Aberdeen's maritime heritage. Everything is covered, from herring fishing and whaling to ship-building and the late 20th-century oil industry. The small ancient rooms combine with state-of-the-art computers, audio-visual technology, artefacts and oral history to bring the past to life.

✚ 79F3
✉ Shiprow
☎ 01224 337700
🕐 Daily 10–5 (from 11 on Sun)
Moderate

*Ship's model and ancient figurehead in Aberdeen's Maritime Museum*

### FISH MARKET AND HARBOUR ⭐⭐

Fishing is still one of the mainstays of the local economy and few sights can compare with the bustling harbour where fishing vessels lie alongside oil-rig supply boats and modern cruise liners. Pay an early morning visit to the fish market to mingle with the buyers and fishermen as thousands of tons of freshly landed fish are bid for then loaded into huge refrigerated trucks to be transported throughout the UK.

✚ 79F3

75

*This unusual looking building was the former home of Provost Skene*

### PROVOST SKENE'S HOUSE   ✪✪
Dating from 1545, Aberdeen's oldest private dwelling house was the home of its provost (mayor), Sir George Skene, from 1676 to 1685, and is preserved almost unchanged. Astonishingly, its luminous religious paintings survived Reformation zeal to obliterate popish imagery and years of neglect. Finally, as a slum threatened with demolition, it was saved to become a museum in 1953. It provides a faithful representation of life for the comfortable burghers of Aberdeen in the late 17th century.

### SATROSPHERE SCIENCE CENTRE   ✪✪✪
This is the only permanent interactive exhibition of Science and Technology in Scotland and a great place to take children. There are no 'DO NOT TOUCH' signs. The message is – do, touch, look, feel. About 80 of the 150 exhibits and experiments are on display at any one time. You can find out about the geological formation of northeast Scotland, marvel at the industry and organisation inside a beehive then compare it with a colony of ants, guess what the mystery sticky liquids are, test the speed of your reactions, experience the Satrosphere's very own black hole and much, much more. Fascinating for visitors of all ages, it may trigger a lifelong interest in science.

### TOLBOOTH MUSEUM   ✪✪
The Tolbooth Museum, within the granite Town House, was the town gaol in 17th-century Aberdeen. The claustrophobic narrow staircases and cramped cells chillingly evoke the grim existence of prisoners here. An audio-visual display and a lifelike model of a prisoner tell tales of the wretched life and of escapes from the bleak conditions.

# What to See in the North

### BALLATER AND BALMORAL ✪✪

Balmoral, a fine example of Scottish Baronial architecture, was converted to a private residence for Queen Victoria in 1855 and became a favourite summer residence for the Royal Family. The local shops in Ballater flaunt their 'By Royal Appointment' signs. The town is a grand base for exploring the area, and Balmoral Estate hires out ponies for pony trekking.

✚ 79E2
✉ Balmoral Estate: 13km (8 miles) west of Ballater on the A93
☎ 013397 42334
🕐 Mid-Apr to end Jul, daily 10–5. Closed Sun in Apr
🍴 Refreshments (£)
✋ Moderate

### BETTYHILL ✪

The tiny coastal village of Bettyhill, at the centre of the local crofting community, suffered mass emigration during the Highland Clearances. The tiny **Strathnaver Museum**, in the former church, tells the story of some of the most horrific evictions, ordered by Elizabeth, Countess of Sutherland. Ironically the village was named after her. Near by are two of the whitest sand beaches in Britain and the Invernaver Nature Reserve, where otters and Arctic terns can often be spotted.

✚ 79D5

**Strathnaver Museum**
✉ In the old church
☎ 01641 521418
🕐 Apr–Oct, Mon–Sat 10–1, 2–5 (and by arrangement)
✋ Cheap

### THE CAIRNGORMS ✪✪

Within the area of this range of mountains, outdoor enthusiasts can find skiing, canoeing, mountaineering, cycling and walking and a rich variety of flora and fauna. The 40km (25 miles) of the Lairig Ghru, running through a majestic mountain pass from Aviemore to Braemar, are reputed to be the best walk in Scotland, although its unpredictable weather and biting cold can test the endurance of the most experienced walker. However, there are lots of shorter, less demanding walks in this glorious landscape. Aviemore village is ideal for exploring the area and its numerous shops sell and rent equipment. Nearby Loch Morlich Watersports and the Scottish National Sports Council's Glenmore Lodge provide facilities and training.

✚ 79D3
ℹ Grampian Road, Aviemore ☎ 01479 810363 🕐 Mon–Sat 9–5

*The majestic Cairngorms offer some of Scotland's finest walking*

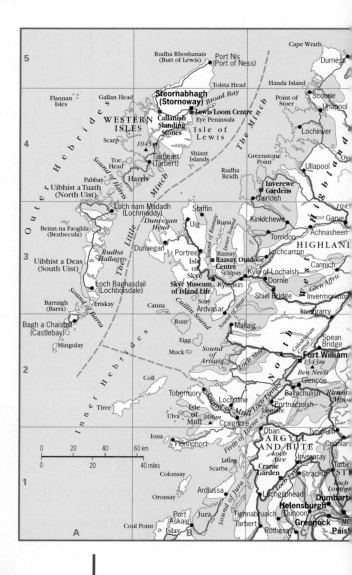

# NORTHERN SCOTLAND

*Pentland Firth*
Dunnet Head
Island of Stroma
Duncansby Head
John O'Groats
Thurso
Castletown
Strathy Point
Melvich
Whiten Head
Bettyhill
Tongue
Noss Head
Wick

Altnaharra
Kinbrace
Latheron

*Loch*
*Shin*
Lairg
Helmsdale

Bonar Bridge
Dornoch
Tarbat Ness
*Dornoch Firth*
Tain

Invergordon
Cromarty
*Moray Firth*
Lossiemouth
Buckie
Cullen
Banff
Macduff
Kinnaird Head
Fraserburgh

Dingwall
Nairn
Forres
Elgin
Keith
Turriff
Peterhead
Fort George
Cawdor Castle
MORAY
Aberlour
Huntly
Ellon
Inverness
Culloden Battlefield
Drumnadrochit
*Spey*
Grantown-on-Spey
Rhynie
Tomatin
Tomintoul
*Don*
Alford

*Monadhliath Mountains*
Aviemore
Rothiemurchus
*The Cairngorms*
ABERDEENSHIRE
ABERDEEN CITY
Aberdeen

Kingussie
Newtonmore
Balmoral Castle
Ballater
*Dee*
Banchory
Braemar
*Grampian Mountains*
Dalwhinnie
Stonehaven

PERTH AND KINROSS
Pitlochry
*Angus Glens*
ANGUS
Brechin
Montrose
Aberfeldy
Kirriemuir
Montrose Basin Wildlife Centre
*Lunan Bay*
Blairgowrie
Forfar
Arbroath
Killin
Dunkeld
Coupar Angus
*Loch Tay*
Scone Palace
DUNDEE CITY
Carnoustie
Lochearnhead
Dundee
Newport-on-Tay
Crieff
Kinfauns
*Firth of Tay*
Perth
Cupar
St Andrews
*The Trossachs*
Callander
Bridge of Earn
M90
Kinross
Crail
Doune
FIFE
Elie *East Neuk of Fife*
STIRLING
Dunblane
Glenrothes
*Loch Leven*
Buckhaven
Stirling
M9
Kincardine
Kirkcaldy
North Berwick
Dunfermline
Cowdenbeath
Falkirk
Bo'ness
Linlithgow
*Firth of Forth*
EDINBURGH
M73
M8
Livingston
Musselburgh
St Abb's Head
GLASGOW
Dalkeith
Eyemouth

✚ 78C2

**Clansmen's Centre**
✉ On the banks of the canal in Fort Augustus
☎ 01320 366444
🕐 Apr, May, Jun, Sep 11–5; Jul, Aug 10–6
👆 Cheap

*Fishing boat moored on the Caledonian Canal*

---

✚ 79D3
✉ Cawdor
☎ 01667 404615
🕐 May–Oct, daily 10–5
🍴 Restaurant (££) and picnic areas
👆 Expensive

---

✚ 79D3

**Cromarty Courthouse**
✉ Church Street
☎ 01381 600418
🕐 Apr–Oct, daily 10–5; Nov, Dec, Mar noon–4
👆 Moderate

## CALEDONIAN CANAL AND THE GREAT GLEN

One of Thomas Telford's greatest engineering achievements was the Caledonian Canal linking lochs Ness, Oich, Lochy and Linnhe from Inverness in the east to Fort William in the west. A slow boat through the Great Glen, watching the reflection of forest greenery or massed broom along the banks is a tranquil and awesome experience. For the more energetic there are lots of off-road walking or cycling trails on disused military roads, the old railway line or the towpath. At Fort Augustus, the **Clansmen's Centre** illustrates 17th-century clan life in a reconstructed turf house.

## CAWDOR CASTLE

Shakespeare's chilling tale had the 12th-century Thane of Cawdor, Macbeth, murder King Duncan in Cawdor Castle. In fact the Cawdor family, who still live here, did not build this fairy-tale castle until the 14th century. According to legend it was built around a thorn tree, still on view in the Thorn Room. The extensive grounds are delightful, including nature walks, a walled garden and the winding Cawdor burn.

## CROMARTY

Cromarty is a picturesque village on the northeast coast of the Black Isle. The local museum in the old **courthouse** and the thatched cottage of Hugh Miller's birthplace between them bring the varied past of this little port vividly to life. You can take a boat trip to watch dolphins, porpoises and even, on occasion, killer whales. However, the massive oil rigs of Nigg and Invergordon cannot be ignored, dominating the Cromarty Firth by day and lighting up the night.

**CULLODEN BATTLEFIELD (▶ 18, TOP TEN)**

## DORNOCH ✪

In 1722 Dornoch was the last place in Scotland to burn a witch. To the south of the town square, the Witch's Stone is a reminder of the poor soul who was roasted in a barrel of tar for allegedly turning her daughter into a pony. The centre-piece of the square is the tiny cathedral, all but destroyed in the 16th century and extensively rebuilt in the 19th century, incorporating skulls and coffins and other intimations of mortality.

✝ 79D4
ℹ The Square ☎ 01862 810400 ⏰ All year

## FORT GEORGE ✪

After the rout of Bonnie Prince Charlie's Highland army at Culloden in 1746, the Hanoverians embarked on a drastic plan for subduing 'rebellious Scots'. One measure was the construction of Fort George, on a spit running into the Moray Firth. It continues as an army barracks to this day and is the home of the **Regimental Museum of the Queen's Own Highlanders**. Allow half a day to visit. The walk along the ramparts is a mile.

✝ 79D3
✉ B9039, off the A96 west of Nairn

**Regimental Museum of the Queen's Own Highlanders**
☎ 01667 462800 ext 8701
⏰ Apr–Sep, Mon–Sat 10–6, Sun 2–6; winter, Mon–Fri 10–4 💷 Moderate

## GLEN AFFRIC ✪✪✪

As well as having some of the most serious walking, Glen Affric is undoubtedly one of the most beautiful glens in Scotland, with stretches of lovely lochs and forestry. The abundance of birch, pine and alder which grace the glen, is a glorious sight in blazing autumn colours. It has one of the most remote youth hostels in Britain, requiring a hike of several miles to reach it. Day-trippers can just picnic or delight in the scenery.

✝ 78C3
✉ Southwest of Cannich, off the A831

*The Dog Falls in scenic Glen Affric*

**GLEN COE (➤ 20–1, TOP TEN)**

**INVEREWE GARDENS** ✪✪

The Gulf Stream flows around the west coast of Scotland producing a warm temperate climate, ideal for gardens. Inverewe was created between 1862 and 1922 by the estate owner, Osgood Mackenzie. The garden has spilled out from its original walled enclave to cover the peninsula. Scots pine, birch, oak and rowan stand alongside semi-tropical exotic plants in a series of delightful small gardens, interconnected by miles of paths.

---

🞤 78C4
✉ Poolewe
☎ 01445 781200
🕐 Daily 9:30–sunset
🍴 Restaurant (£)
👜 Moderate

*Shrubs and trees at Inverewe Gardens*

---

**INVERNESS** ✪✪

Inverness is an attractive town, built mainly in the 19th century, with a fine cathedral and castle. Situated on the Moray Firth at the eastern end of the Caledonian Canal, it is the largest town in the Highlands, an important transport hub and the best base for exploring the area.

---

🞤 79D3
ℹ Castle Wynd ☎ 01463 234353 🕐 All year

---

**KINGUSSIE** ✪✪

Kingussie, a typical small town built round a single main street, is an oasis of tranquillity bypassed by the hurly-burly of the main artery north, the A9. At the **Highland Folk Museum** you can explore reconstructions of a Lewis black house (a traditional Hebridean low stone dwelling with thatched roof), a salmon smoking shed and a water mill, as well as finding out everything there is to know about the history of the area. Near by the ruins of Ruthven Barracks stand proud and roofless against the skyline. They were part of the fortifications built to ensure stability in the

---

🞤 78D2

**Highland Folk Museum**
✉ Duke Street
☎ 01540 661307
🕐 Mar–May and Sep–Oct, Mon–Fri 10:30–4:30 (guided tours only); Jun–Aug, Mon–Sat 10:30–5, Sun 1–5
👜 Moderate

region after the Jacobite Rebellion of 1745. From Ruthven you can walk a surviving stretch of General Wade's military road, crossing a perfectly preserved example of a Wade bridge near Dalwhinnie.

## LOCH NESS ✪✪✪
The world-famous loch is forever linked to its resident beastie, the Loch Ness Monster. The loch is long and deep and swarming with Nessie spotters. At Drumnadrochit there are two monster centres: the Original Loch Ness Monster Exhibition, and the considerably better **Official Loch Ness Exhibition Centre**.

Castle Urquhart, a couple of miles south, is the best monster spotting site, where most of the Nessie photographs have been taken. The ruins of the 14th-century castle themselves are worth a visit. Perched atop a rocky cliff the castle was of strategic importance in guarding the Great Glen. It was destroyed in 1692 to prevent its use by the Jacobites.

## ROTHIEMURCHUS ✪
The huge estate of Rothiemurchus, belonging to the Grant family, extends from the village of Aviemore to the Cairngorm plateaux. The lovely woodlands here, with the Cairngorms forming a backdrop, are particularly noted for their magnificent Caledonian pine. From the estate visitors' centre, there's access to a superb mountain bike track and miles of footpaths through forests, over heather moorlands and by lochs and rivers. There is also a nature trail around Loch an Eilean and other activities include clay-pigeon shooting, ranger walks and fishing on the Spey.

*Castle Urquhart, Loch Ness. The perfect location for a spot of monster hunting*

---

➕ 79D3

**Official Loch Ness Exhibition Centre**
✉ Drumnadrochit
☎ 01456 450573
🕐 Daily Nov–Mar 10–4; Easter–May and Oct 9:30–5:30; Jun and Sep 9:30–6:30; Jul and Aug 9–8:30
🎟 Expensive

---

➕ 79D3
✉ 1.5km (1 mile) southeast from Aviemore on the Ski Road
☎ 01479 810858
🕐 Daily 9–5:30
🍴 Tea room (£)
🎟 Free

*Jarlshof, Shetland's prehistoric settlement*

# Shetland & Orkney

✚ 29D4, 29C4

These islands were formerly Norwegian, and the Norse influence is still evident in language and customs. Orkney is a few miles off the Scottish mainland, while Shetland is 96km (60 miles) further north. Each one is a scattering of islands, abounding in wildlife, particularly sea birds. In both, the Mainland refers to the main island while the rest of Scotland is known as 'The Sooth'.

> ### DID YOU KNOW?
>
> The islanders of Foula still use the ancient Julian calendar. Initially this was because the island was remote but nowadays they just like to be different. However, they switch to the standard calendar when it suits them, such as New Year, which they can celebrate on two separate dates.

## What to See in Shetland

### FOULA ✪✪

✚ 29D4
🚢 Ferries to Foula from Walls ☎ 01595 753226 for information

About 22km (14 miles) east of the Mainland is Foula, a world apart. Traces of an ancient way of life – peat fires and eking out a subsistence living – cling to this remote island. Until a few years ago, the island schoolteacher was responsible for christenings, marriages and funerals in his role as Church of Scotland missionary. Foula teems with bird life, particularly puffins and great skuas.

### JARLSHOF ✪✪

✚ 29D4
✉ Sumburgh
☎ 01950 460112
🕓 Apr–Sep, daily 9:30–6:30. Phone for winter hours
✋ Cheap

This ancient settlement was inhabited from the Stone Age to the 17th century. There's a broch (round tower made of two layers of stones with stairs built into the thickness of the wall) and a medieval building, but the most interesting dwellings are the Norse longhouses and the complex wheelhouse structures with underground corridors, bedrooms and central hearths.

### LERWICK

Lerwick has an attractive harbour where fishing boats jostle for space alongside transporters for the oil industry and the Greenpeace *Rainbow Warrior*, a frequent visitor. The narrow winding main street runs behind the harbour front and countless tiny alleys climb steeply up the hill.

**Up Helly Aa**, once a pagan fire festival to celebrate the end of the ancient Yule celebration, is now a well organised spectacle in which a thousand men with blazing torches march through the streets of Lerwick. Behind them they drag a Viking galley to the burning ground where they throw their torches into the vessel. If you can't be there to see it in January there is an excellent exhibition with an audio-visual with examples of Viking costumes and pictures of bearded warriors in winged helmets, standing before the burning craft.

✚ 29D4

**Up Helly Aa**
✉ Galley Shed off Sunniva Street
🕐 Mid-May to mid-Sep, Tue 2–4, 7–9, Fri 5–9, Sat 2–4
ℹ Shetland Island Tourism, Market Cross ☎ 01595 693434
✋ Cheap

## What to See in Orkney

### ITALIAN CHAPEL ✪✪✪

Although built from Nissen huts, concrete, barbed wire and paint by Italian POWs in 1943, the love and reverence which went into this exquisite little gem are evident. Artist Domenico Chiocchetti designed the interior, creating *trompe-l'oeil* stonework and windows, and a magnificent fresco altarpiece.

✚ 29C4
✉ Lamb Holm
🕐 Most of the time
✋ Free

### KIRKWALL AND ST MAGNUS CATHEDRAL ✪✪✪

Kirkwall is the largest town in Orkney and the island capital. St Magnus Cathedral, founded by Jarl Rognvlad in 1137 and built over a period of 300 years, has architectural details ranging from Norman to early Gothic. The exquisite carving, the glowing red and yellow stone and its small size give it a strange feeling of delicacy and lightness for a medieval cathedral.

✚ 29C4
ℹ Orkney Tourist Board, 6 Broad Street, Klrkwall ☎ 01856 872856

Above: *a lifeboat in Lerwick harbour*

### MAES HOWE ✪✪✪

This neolithic burial chamber is the finest chambered tomb in Western Europe. You have to creep through a long narrow stone tunnel to reach the central chamber. It was built 4,000 years ago with such precision that the sun lights the tunnel at sunset on midwinter. When opened last century, no treasures were found. Vikings had beaten the Victorians to the plunder, leaving a collection of Runic graffiti which would translate well to lavatory walls today.

✚ 29C4
✉ Stenness
☎ 01856 761606
🕐 Apr–Sep, daily 9:30–6:30; Oct–Mar, Mon–Sat 9:30–4:30, Sun 2–4:30
🍴 Café (£)
✋ Cheap

### SKARA BRAE (▶ 24, TOP TEN)

# Shetland, Mousa Island and Broch

**Distance**
6km (4 miles)

**Time**
3 hours (including ferry)

**Start/end point**
The pier at Leebitton Harbour,
Sandwick
✚ 29D4

**Lunch**
There are no facilities on
Mousa, so take a packed
lunch

*Mousa Broch, an ancient
Pictish fortification*

Mousa is a small, uninhabited island to the east of
Mainland Shetland, with an unrivalled example of a broch –
the circular, fortified, drystone tower of the Iron Age.
Abundant wildlife includes seals and storm petrels, eider
ducks, waders and skuas, which swoop and dive everywhere, unmoved by the approach of humans.

*Turn right from the jetty and follow the path
along the coast to your right until you come to
the broch.*

Built between 100 BC and AD 100, Mousa Broch, featured
in the great Viking Sagas, remains almost intact. A narrow
passage leads to an inner courtyard where the encircling
massive stone wall bears in on you as you look up at the
circle of sky 12m above. Torches are supplied to climb the
narrow, worn stairs in the dark space within the walls. At
the top you can see where great beams would have
supported the turf roof and view a coastline that the
original builders would still recognise.

*Follow the path round the coast from the broch
or head inland with the remains of a house on
your right.*

The map you get from the boatman indicates areas to be
avoided during the nesting season. Either way you will
reach two sheltered bays on the east side where seals
gather. There may be just two or three swimming or
possibly a hundred or so in and out of the water.

*From the bay follow the path back to the jetty
and the small stone cottage that now serves as a
shepherd's bothy.*

# Skye & the Western Isles

This group of islands contain some of the bleakest and most beautiful scenery in Scotland. From the majestic Cuillins of Skye through the flat water-logged moors of North Uist and the rolling hills of Harris to the timeless charm of the smaller islands, Eigg, Muck, Rum, Canna, Barra and Eriskay, you could spend a lifetime exploring here. Walk the ancient paths and hill tracks, seek out secluded bays or visit prehistoric settlements and still there are further delights to uncover.

## What to See in Skye & the Western Isles

### CALLANISH STONES, ISLE OF LEWIS ✪✪✪

Built over 4,000 years ago, and 1,000 years before the pyramids of Egypt, this is possibly the most spectacular and intact prehistoric site in Europe. Standing on a raised site overlooking Loch Roag, the 4.5m-high stones form the shape of a Celtic cross. The main part of the site is a circle of 13 stones with an avenue of 19 monoliths leading north.

🛈 Western Isles Tourist Board, 26 Cromwell Street, Stornoway, Isle of Lewis ☎ 0 851 703088

🛲 78B4
✉ Callanish
☎ 01851 621422
🕐 Apr–Sep, daily 10–7 (closes at 4 in winter)
🍴 Café (£)
👋 Cheap

*The standing stones of Callanish. Once a place of worship or perhaps a prehistoric calendar?*

87

📍 78B4
✉ Old Grainstore, Bayhead Street
☎ 01851 704500
🕐 Apr–Dec, Mon–Sat 9–6
💷 Cheap

*Skye's Cuillin mountains beyond the old bridge at Sligachan*

📍 78B3
✉ Inverarish
☎ 01478 660266
🕐 Accommodation all year, activities Mar–Oct
💷 Expensive

📍 78B3
✉ Near Loch Ainort
☎ 01470 552206
🕐 Apr–Oct, daily 9:30–5:30
🍴 Tea room (£)
💷 Cheap

### LEWIS LOOM CENTRE, ISLE OF LEWIS  ✪✪

Harris tweed production is one of the mainstays of the local economy in the Outer Hebrides and is still woven by hand. The only place in the islands where the entire production process can be seen is the Lewis Loom Centre in Stornoway, where Ronnie Mackenzie has set up a small museum and exhibition centre. Ronnie will demonstrate carding, spinning and warping, and explain about natural and synthetic dyes. Then he'll weave some cloth, talk about waulking the finished material and answer questions. His shop stocks a wide variety of Harris tweed clothing.

### RAASAY OUTDOOR CENTRE, RAASAY  ✪✪

Raasay is the place for anyone looking for an adventure sport holiday. The centre provides equipment and instruction for a bewildering array of activities including sailing, water-skiing, sailboarding, mountain biking, walking and climbing. Accommodation is provided in the house where Dr Samuel Johnstone (1709–84), a leading journalist and literary figure, and his biographer, James Boswell (1704–95), lodged during their tour of the Hebrides. The activities are open to day visitors, too.

### SKYE MUSEUM OF ISLAND LIFE, ISLE OF SKYE  ✪✪✪

This 'living museum' is a series of seven thatched black houses, reconstructed to form an ancient island township. The original black house on the site is much as it was when it was last inhabited in the late 1950s. Here locals re-create the crofting way of life as it was a century ago. Behind the museum is the grave of Flora MacDonald who helped Bonnie Prince Charlie to escape the Hanoverian forces after his defeat at Culloden.

# Harris & Lewis

This coastal drive round the islands of Lewis and Harris takes in the most important attractions in the Hebrides.

*From Stornoway take the A859 towards Tarbert which is 56km (35 mile) away on Harris. Continue on the A859 to Leverburgh. From Leverburgh continue on the A859 as far as Rodel, then follow the local road as it meanders along the east coast via Manish to rejoin the A859 south of Tarbert.*

Called the Golden Highway, because of the expense of building it, this is a winding, single track road with passing places. It connects a number of small remote settlements strung out across a land which resembles a moonscape – rugged, rocky, empty and painfully beautiful.

*From Tarbert drive back towards Stornoway on the A859. At Leurbost, turn left on the local road which links with the A858 at Achmore. Follow this road to Callanish.*

The standing stones of Callanish (► 87), constructed about a thousand years before the pyramids, stand above Loch Roag.

*Continue on the road past Carloway, Arnol and through Barvas to Lional, then follow the signs for the Butt of Lewis.*

| Greosabhagh | $1\frac{1}{2}$ |
| (Scadabhagh | 4) |
| Collam | $2\frac{1}{2}$ |
| Cliuthar | 3 |
| Stocinis | 4 |
| Leac a Li | 5 |

Carloway Broch is worth a visit, and the nearby village of Garenin with its restored black houses should not be missed. Arnol Black House was built in 1885 and served continuously as a dwelling until 1964. The young woman who lived there with her mother is now the caretaker/guide.

*From the lighthouse at the Butt of Lewis return by the same route as far as Barvas then turn left on to the A857 to Stornoway.*

**Distance**
298km (185 miles)

**Time**
6–8 hours depending on stops

**Start/end point**
Stornoway
⊹ 28A4

**Lunch**
Harris Hotel, Tarbert (££)
☎ 01859 502154

*Road signs in the Western Isles are in Gaelic*

78 C4
Argyle Street ☎ 01854 612135 🅒 Easter–Nov, Mon–Fri 9–6, Sun 1–6

**Leckmelm Shrubbery and Arboretum**
✉ 5km (3 miles) south of Ullapool on A835
☎ 0131 229 1870 (Scottish Gardens Scheme)
🕓 May–Sep 10–6
💷 Cheap

*The tiny houses of Ullapool stretch out along the shores of Loch Broom*

## ULLAPOOL ✪✪

Ullapool, at the head of Loch Broom, was built as a planned fishing village in 1788 by the British Fisheries Society. Today, it is still a bustling fishing port, as well as the ferry terminal for the Western Isles and the main base for exploring Wester Ross. It has a lively cultural centre at the Ceilidh Place (➤ 38), where people can enjoy the outdoors by day and sample live traditional music and dancing in the evening. The surrounding countryside abounds in walks such as the old drove road to Loch Achall and back over the summit of Meall Mor, with a breath-taking view over Loch Broom and the Summer Isles.

The Isles are a small group of uninhabited islands accessible by boat from Ullapool and Achiltibuie during the summer months. Most trips allow an hour on shore on Tanera Mhor, the largest island in the group. As well as sea birds, you are likely to see seals, dolphins and porpoises. Five kilometres (3 miles) from Ullapool on Loch Broom, you will find **Leckmelm Shrubbery and Arboretum**, dating from the 1870s, which is renowned for its rare trees and plants, including rhododendrons and azaleas.

Corrieshalloch Gorge, on the A835 south of Ullapool, is a 1.5km- (1-mile) long, 60m-deep box canyon with an information board which tells you all about its geological and botanical interest. However, it's the Falls of Measach that most people come to see. The 45m cascade can be viewed from a narrow suspension bridge that spans the gorge or from the observation platform.

# Where To...

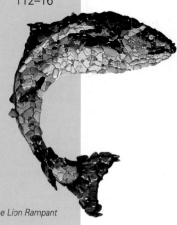

Above: *the flags of Scotland – the Lion Rampant and the Saltire*
Right: *this fish design is on a window in the Scottish Fisheries Museum at Anstruther*

# Edinburgh & the Borders

## Prices

Approximate prices for a three-course meal, excluding wine, for one person are shown by the £ symbol:

£   = under £15
££  = £15–25
£££ = over £25

## Edinburgh

### Atrium (£££)

Mediterranean meets Midlothian is one way to describe the menu here. Try the Cullen skink, a type of fish soup, and the black pudding and mushroom pasta.

✉ Cambridge Street ☎ 0131 228 8882

### Caledonian Hotel (£–£££)

Chisholms restaurant serves brasserie-style food all day. Particularly popular is their haggis, neeps and tatties which you can have as a starter or main course. The Pompadour restaurant was undergoing a major refurbishment at the time of writing but it is likely to re-establish itself as one of the premier eating places in the capital.

✉ Princes Street ☎ 0131 459 9988

### Channings Hotel (££)

A blend of Scottish and European cooking, a feature of many Edinburgh restaurants, is the speciality of The Brasserie. Try, in particular, the freshly baked bread and the scallops and spring onions.

✉ South Learmonth Gardens ☎ 0131 315 2226

### George Inter-Continental (£££)

Le Chambertin is an intimate French restuarant where the quality of the food is matched by the enthusiasm of the staff. Ask for a window seat looking out on to the Georgian New Town and let the sommelier recommend a wine.

✉ 19–21 George Street ☎ 0131 225 1251

### Lo Stado (£)

Family-run Italian café/bar where the food is freshly cooked from quality ingredients. The all-day breakfast and children's menus are very popular.

✉ North Bridge Street ☎ 0131 225 9038

### Sheraton Grand (£££)

Classic French and Scottish cuisine. Particularly good for seafood such as salmon, scallops and roast sea bass. The wine list has got to be seen to be believed.

✉ 1 Festival Square ☎ 0131 221 9131

### Winter Glen (££)

Blair Glen and Graham Winter's magic basement restaurant where Graham produces great Scottish cooking and a very wicked warm chocolate cake.

✉ 3A1 Dundas Street ☎ 0131 477 7060

### The Witchery and Secret Garden (££)

This is the best eating experience in Edinburgh. The light, airy Secret Garden with its tapestry-hung stone walls downstairs and the atmospheric, candle-lit, Witchery, combine with the best in Scottish cuisine and desserts to die for.

✉ 352 Castle Hill, Royal Mile ☎ 0131 225 5613

## The Borders

### Biggar

#### Shieldhill Hotel (££)

Daily changing menu which features delights such as chicken, spinach and tomato roulade with herb salad and walnut oil. No smoking.

✉ Quothquan ☎ 01899 220035

## Chirnside
### Chirnside Hall (££)
The dining-room has grand views over the surrounding countryside and offers seasonal dishes such as poached monkfish served with a tartlet of langoustine and crisp-edged duckling with a honey and soy sauce, prepared from quality Scottish produce.
✉ **On the A6105 Berwick-upon-Tweed/Duns road** ☎ **01890 818219**

## Gullane
### Greywalls Hotel (£££)
Set four-course dinner in a dining-room overlooking Muirfield golf course, serving Aberdeen Angus beef, Loch Fyne smoked salmon and local lamb and cheeses. The ideal place to treat yourself.
✉ **Muirfield** ☎ **01620 842144**

### La Potinière (££)
Dinner at weekends only, but lunch is served all week. Very popular and needs to be booked well in advance, but well worth the effort.
✉ **Main Street** ☎ **01620 843214**

## Kelso
### Sunlaws House Hotel (££)
This is the Duke of Roxburgh's place and very popular with the huntin', fishin' and shootin' set. The Duke's estate supplies the Tweed salmon and wild game featured on the menu.
✉ **Heiton (5km/3 miles southwest of Kelso on the A698)** ☎ **01573 450331**

## Kirknewton
### Marriot Dalmahoy Hotel (££)
A plush place where guests are expected to wear a jacket and tie. The Pentland Restaurant overlooks the 18th hole of the golf course. Very good food as well.
✉ **On the A71, 3km (2 miles) east of Kirknewton** ☎ **0131 333 1845**

## Linlithgow
### Champany Inn (£££, lunch, ££)
An old mill house dating from the time of Mary, Queen of Scots, and with a long-standing reputation for quality Scottish dishes.
✉ **3km (2 miles) northeast** ☎ **01506 834532**

## Melrose
### Burt's Hotel (££)
Burt's, famous for its beef obtained from quality-assured farms, is a member of the Scotch Beef Club. The modern menu also features dishes such as chicken and sausage haggis and a lasagne of salmon and halibut served with ratatouille.
✉ **Market Square** ☎ **01896 822285**

## Peebles
### Cringletie House Hotel (£££)
Regional produce used extensively in an imaginative way to produce such delights as courgette and rosemary soup with crème fraiche.
✉ **3km (2 miles) north on the A703** ☎ **01721 730233**

## Swinton
### Wheatsheaf Hotel (££)
Small hotel on the village green. The menu features wood pigeon, duck and corn-fed chicken.
✉ **Main Street** ☎ **01890 860257**

### Stovies
This is surely the food of the gods. Originally the poor person's stew made with very little meat and a lot of potatoes and vegetables, the recipe and contents vary by locality and preference. Nowadays you'll find it on the menus of some pubs and in snack bars. Fresco at 223 Canongate, Edinburgh ☎ 0131 556 6077, serves some of the best.

# Glasgow & the Southwest

### Deep Fried Mars Bars

This rather dubious Scottish delicacy is on sale in fish and chip shops throughout the land. Take one Mars bar, cover with batter, deep fry in hot oil for a few minutes then serve with chips. Tasty it is. Healthy it is not, and it's little wonder that Glasgow is the heart attack capital of Europe with this one on the menu.

*SCOTIA CAFE FOR DRINKS & MUSIC* (handwritten note)

## Glasgow

### Buttery Restaurant (£££)

More of an experience than a restaurant. Underneath the Kingston Bridge, this former corner pub has survived intact amid new housing. Step through the door and you are back in Victorian times, staff in period clothes and white gloves. The gantry in the bar is magnificent and there are bottles of cologne in the toilets. The food is pretty special too – Highland venison layered with redcurrants and apple chutney and warm banana crêpe with chocolate sauce.

✉ 652 Argyle Street ☎ 0141 221 8188

### Glasgow Hilton (£££)

Several restaurants in the Glasgow Hilton, including Camerons, serve prime Scottish food and a wine list that can cater to the most discerning of palates.

✉ 1 Williams Street ☎ 0141 204 5555

### Glasgow Moat House (££)

Another large city-centre hotel with several choices of restaurant serving informal meals to fine dining. The seafood is very tasty.

✉ Congress Road ☎ 0141 306 9988

### Killermont Polo Club (££)

In a city with many Indian restaurants the Killermont Polo Club offers consistent quality coupled with friendly service.

✉ 2002 Maryhill Road, Maryhill Park ☎ 0141 946 5412

### Nairns (££)

Celebrity chef Nick Nairn's new place situated in a smart town house providing top-notch food at affordable prices. The set-price menu is very good value.

✉ 13 Woodside Crescent ☎ 0141 353 0707

### La Parmigiana (££)

Locals, who should know a good deal, have supported this trattoria for years. The baked sea bass with a lemon butter sauce is tasty, as are the classic Italian dishes.

✉ 447 Great Western Road ☎ 0141 334 0686

### Ubiquitous Chip (£–££)

Wonderful, popular restaurant and bistro near the University. The Scottish menu is served in the verdant courtyard restaurant or in the upstairs balcony.

✉ 12 Ashton Lane, Hillhead ☎ 0141 334 5007

### Yes (£££)

Light, pleasant, downstairs restaurant serving delightfully prepared Scottish food. Particularly good is the Buccleuch beef, and the freshly baked bread with olive oil is for those of us who don't care about calories. Vegetarians are very well catered for here.

✉ 22 West Nile Street ☎ 0141 221 8044

## The Southwest

### Ayr

#### Fairfield House Hotel (££)

Timbale of smoked salmon filled with a lobster and sweet red pepper bavarois, and roast monkfish tails on a parsnip and potato cake with fresh pesto are just two of the mouth-watering seafood dishes on the menu.

✉ 12 Fairfield Road ☎ 01292 267461

### Fouters Bistro (£–££)
Laurie Black has been at Fouters for 25 years. His interpretation of modern Scottish cooking makes this restaurant one of the most popular eating places in Ayrshire.

✉ **2A Academy Street**
☎ **01292 261391**

## Gatehouse of Fleet
### Cally Palace Hotel (£££)
Simple and honest is how this grand hotel describes its dishes. Good Scottish fare based on local produce and prepared to the highest standard.

✉ **1.5km (1 mile) from Gatehouse** ☎ **01557 814341**

## Girvan
### Wildings (££)
This small fishing town restaurant has been around for many years in several guises, each one an improvement on the last. Chef, Kevin Rae, puts the emphasis on locally landed seafood, prawns, scallops, hake and salmon.

✉ **Montgomerie Street**
☎ **01465 713481**

## Moffat
### Beechwood Country House Hotel (££)
Pleasant wooded surroundings and a Victorian house provide the ambience in which to enjoy a regularly changing menu in a non-smoking dining-room.

✉ **Harthorpe Place** ☎ **01683 220210**

## Moniaive
### Craigdarroch Arms (£)
This very old, family-run hotel has an awesome reputation for the quality of its food. Ranging from inexpensive bar snacks, served by a blazing log fire in the lounge, to a full restaurant menu with such delights as pan-seared ostrich steaks and the famed Craigdarroch mixed grill.

✉ **High Street** ☎ **01848 200205**

## Newton Stewart
### Kirroughtree House (£££)
Duck with potatoes, celeriac purée, black pudding and ratatouille may sound like a terrible mixture but wait till you see how they are combined to create one of the mouth-watering dishes the hotel is famous for.

✉ **Minnigaff** ☎ **01671 402141**

## Portpatrick
### Knockinaam Lodge Hotel (£££)
Gourmet meals prepared from fresh local ingredients served in a Victorian hunting lodge facing the Irish Sea.

✉ **East of Portpatrick off the A77** ☎ **01776 810471**

## Troon
### Highgrove House (£££)
Sitting on a hillside with stupendous views over the Firth of Clyde is one of the plus points of Highgrove House. Scottish cuisine using produce from all over the country, prepared in an imaginative and innovative manner is another.

✉ **Old Loans Road** ☎ **01292 312511**

## Turnberry
### Turnberry Hotel (£££)
If you can't afford to stay at the hotel at the very least treat yourself to a meal here, or perhaps afternoon tea.

✉ **Just north of the village on the A719** ☎ **01655 331000**

### Square Slice
Made from ground meat, breadcrumbs and spice, this excellent sausage, peculiar to Scotland, is formed into a long square loaf and cut into slices. Its proper name is Lorne Sausage, but no one calls it that. Try it fried for breakfast or in a bun or sandwich with an optional topping of a fried egg and fried tattie (potato) scone.

# Central Scotland

**Selkirk Bannocks**
Although this mouth-watering cake can be bought throughout Scotland, the best ones will be found in the Scottish Borders. They're large, flat, round loaves made by adding butter, sugar and fruit to bread dough. Then they're baked on a gridle or in the oven. Look for the ones made from the original recipe.

## Anstruther
### Cellar Restaurant (££)
This used to be a cooperage where barrels were made for the herring industry. Now herrings are served to the customers along with a wide variety of other fish, East Neuk crab and meat.
✉ **24 East Green** ☎ **01333 310378**

## Arduaine
### Loch Melfort Hotel (£££)
Sit in the dining-room gazing out over Loch Melfort to the Sound of Jura and you'll forget all about food. Until it arrives that is. Splendid, mouth-watering fare based on local seafood. Be sure to try the disgustingly decadent bread-and-butter pudding.
✉ **On the A816 midway between Oban and Lochgilphead** ☎ **01852 200233**

## Auchterarder
### The Gleneagles Hotel (£££)
One of Scotland's finest hotels offering some of the country's finest cooking. Soufflé created from Lanark blue cheese and pine nuts, chargrilled quail and smoked venison are just a few of the dishes guaranteed to get the juices flowing.
✉ **On A823** ☎ **01764 662231**

## Balloch
### Cameron House Hotel (££–£££)
Sitting on the Bonnie Banks of Loch Lomond looking out on to Inchmurrin island and Ben Lomond, this hotel offers a choice of three restaurants, including the bar-diner in the nearby marina or the fine Georgian Room in the hotel.
✉ **Loch Lomond** ☎ **01389 755565**

## Balquhidder
### Monachyle Mhor (££)
Right in the heart of Rob Roy country and the romantic Braes of Balquhidder, the dining-room overlooks two lochs. Tom Lewis is a chef/proprietor who really understands food and how it should be cooked.
✉ **Off the A84, south of Lochearnhead** ☎ **01877 384622**

## Killiecrankie
### Killiecrankie Hotel (££)
Pudding wines by the glass are a perfect reason for dining here. Or choose from the dessert list – the white chocolate delice is superb, as is the glazed lemon tart.
✉ **Take A9 north of Pitlochry, left on to B8019 before Killiecrankie** ☎ **01796 473220**

## Lundin Links
### Old Manor Hotel (££)
Modern British cooking, such as sautéed chicken livers with walnut mayonnaise and croutons, is served here.
✉ **Leven Road** ☎ **01333 320368**

## Oban
### Manor House Hotel (££)
Daily changing set menu is very much 'Auld Alliance' fare with Scottish ingredients getting the French treatment.
✉ **Gallanach Road** ☎ **01631 562087**

## Peat Inn
### Peat Inn (£££)
David Wilson has made the Peat Inn a watchword for superb cuisine locally and much further afield. Standing at the crossroads of a small hamlet not far from St Andrews it is *the* place to eat in Fife.

✉ **10km (6 miles) southwest of St Andrews at junction of the B940/B941** ☎ **01334 840206**

## Perth
### Huntingtower Hotel (££)
Reasonable fixed-price menu including creations such as a warm salad of seared scallops and rack of lamb with rosemary and mustard crust are served in the panelled restaurant of a country house hotel.

✉ **Crieff Road, Almondbank** ☎ **01738 583771**

### Kinfauns Castle (£££)
Early 17th-century castle with late 20th-century, award-winning chef makes this one of the most sought-after restaurants in the country. The Scottish Gourmet Evenings rank as essential eating.

✉ **Kinfauns** ☎ **01738 620777**

### Number Thirty Three Seafood Restaurant (££)
Mussels with Camembert, cheese scone served with olive bread and home-made ice-cream complement a range of fish dishes.

✉ **33 George Street** ☎ **01738 633771**

## Pitlochry
### Knockendarroch House Hotel (££)
Victorian mansion looking over the Tummel Valley offers a set menu with two choices for each course. Try the fish in beer batter sauce and the rhubarb crumble.

✉ **Higher Oakfield** ☎ **01796 473473**

## St Andrews
### The Old Course Hotel (£££)
Dine well while looking over the famous Old Course.

Caesar salad, crispy Cajun onion rings and red fish with *bok choi* sit comfortably on the menu with Scottish beef and fish.

✉ **40 The Scores** ☎ **01334 474371**

### Rufflets (££)
The Garden Restaurant in this turreted mansion is an absolute pleasure. Local ingredients are combined with imagination to produce such delights as Brie baked with prosciutto in oatmeal, white grilled collops of Rannoch venison in a port and pickled walnut jus and an exquisite chocolate parfait with a delicate balance of flavours with crème anglaise and coffee. There is a great wine list, too. with seven sold by the glass.

✉ **Strathkinness Low Road** ☎ **01334 478703**

## Stirling
### Royal Hotel (££)
This Victorian hotel features a stylish restaurant serving such gems as haggis-stuffed chicken with a Drambuie sauce, scallops with saffron butter, followed by chocolate marquise with caramel sauce. The Sunday lunches are grand.

✉ **Henderson Street, Bridge of Allan** ☎ **01786 832284**

## Taynuilt
### Taychreggan Hotel (£££)
Once this was a drovers' inn on the north shore of Loch Awe, now it serves great Scottish food in a fixed-price, five-course menu with at least five choices of main course.

✉ **From the A85 take the B845 at Taynuilt to Kilchrenan and Taychreggan** ☎ **01866 833211**

### High Tea
Once ubiquitous, this distinctly Scottish meal has fallen from fashion but can still be found in some old family-run hotels and restaurants. Typically it consists of bread and butter and an old-fashioned three-tiered cake stand piled high with scones, pancakes, shortbread and dreadfully fattening cakes, all washed down with copious quantities of tea.

# The North

## Forfar Bridies

Forfar is the home of the Bridie, a meat-filled flaky pastry which can be purchased from most Scottish bakers. Avoid the supermarket varieties. They vary in texture and quality but if you want to experience the genuine article seek out one of the Forfar bakers who still make them – huge, meaty and very tasty.

## Aberdeen
### Ardoe House (£££)

Five-course gourmet dinners are the speciality of the house, served in the wood-panelled splendour of a baronial mansion.

✉ **South Deeside Road, Blairs**
☎ **01224 867355**

### Simpson's Hotel (££)

Opulent splendour where East meets East Coast. Moroccan columns support a colonnade of arches, flanking a palm court, complete with fountain, leading to a sweeping staircase. The food's 'nae bad' as well with Scottish ingredients such as black pudding and scallops given the Mediterranean treatment.

✉ **59 Queens Road** ☎ **01224 327777**

## Ballater
### Balgonie House Hotel (£££)

Crêpes Suzette, Scottish cheeses and meat on garlic potatoes form a small part of the eclectic menu in this fine Edwardian house. Superb bread as well.

✉ **Braemar Place** ☎ **013397 55482**

### Green Inn (££)

An innovative selection of Scottish dishes with cosmopolitan flavours. Try the Scotch beef and Yorkshire pudding, but don't miss the iced Cranachan mousse.

✉ **9 Victoria Road** ☎ **01339 755701**

## Dufftown
### Taste of Speyside (£)

An absolute cracker. Cullen skink is on the menu, traditional clootie dumpling (➤ side panel), topped with Drambuie cream and a host of local specialities including smoked venison. Round it all off with a glass of malt bearing the same name as the street.

✉ **10 Balvenie Street**
☎ **01340 820860**

## Fort William
### Crannog Restaurant (££)

Converted from an old fisherman's gear shed, this restaurant sits out on the pier. Naturally they serve seafood, mostly local.

✉ **Town Pier** ☎ **01397 705589**

## Glamis
### Castleton House Hotel (££)

Country house with 700-year-old moat. Try the fine chocolate and walnut cheesecake preceded, perhaps, with the fillet of pork, roast shallots and basil tagliatelle. Also bar food.

✉ **Forfar** ☎ **01307 840340**

## Inverness
### Café 1 (£)

French bistro classics meet contemporary British. Try liver and bacon with an onion marmalade and potatoes and parsnip mash followed by a selection of French and Scottish cheeses all washed down with a glass or three of wine.

✉ **76 Castle Street** ☎ **01463 226200**

## Kingussie
### The Cross (£££)

Tony and Ruth Hadley run this converted tweed mill. Tony collects wine with his list extending to more than 400 bins and he knows what he's talking about. The five-course dinner menu features dishes such as fillet of

Highland lamb with Madeira and tarragon, boudin of scallops with asparagus and oriental marinated quail. Just reading the menu is enough to make your mouth water.

✉ **Tweed Mill Brae, Ardbroilach Road** ☎ **01540 661166**

## Muir of Ord
### The Dower House (££)
The fixed-price dinner is a bargain and the wines are reasonably priced in this small and intimate dining-room, but being close to Inverness and very popular, advance booking is essential.

✉ **Highfield** ☎ **01463 870090**

## Onich
### Allt-nan-Ros Hotel (£££)
Good fixed-price dinner menu full of tasty Scottish ingredients, on the shores of Loch Linnhe looking over to the Morven hills. Mine host wears his kilt, and the waitresses wear long tartan skirts.

✉ **Fort William** ☎ **01855 821210**

## Plockton
### Haven Hotel (££)
Deep in the heart of Hamish Macbeth country, the Haven is in the village, which is the location for the popular TV series. The Haven uses the finest local produce including seafood, salmon, Scottish beef, venison and lamb

✉ **Innes Street** ☎ **01599 544223**

## Portree, Isle of Skye
### Cuillin Hills Hotel (££)
Spectacular views of the Cuillins over Portree Bay are the highlight of an evening here. Built in 1870 as a hunting lodge for the Lord of the Isles, it's now one of the premier eating places on Skye. Specialities may include venison steak with juniper berry, gin and garlic *jus*, and over-roasted pheasant with a green peppercorn whisky sauce.

✉ **Just north of Portree off the A855** ☎ **01478 612003**

## Shieldaig
### Tigh an Eilean Hotel (££)
Scotland is full of splendid restaurants run by chef/proprietors. This one is a corker. Callum Stewart's cooking is simple and uses fresh, quality produce. Try his crab dijonnaise, grilled lamb cutlets or poached salmon hollandaise.

✉ **Off the A896** ☎ **01520 755251**

## Torridon
### Loch Torridon Hotel (£££)
In the past the aristocracy captured all the great locations for castles, mansions and hunting lodges. This one, overlooking the excruciatingly beautiful Loch Torridon, is no exception. Try the lobster with cucumber spaghetti in a lobster and sherry sauce, or deer fillet with juniper and sweated red onions.

✉ **Off the A896, southwest of Kinlochewe** ☎ **01445 791242**

## Ullapool
### Altnaharrie Inn (£££)
Mega-expensive even for the fixed-price five-course dinner but cheap at the price and an experience that will never be forgotten. Telephone from Ullapool and the hotel boat will collect you from the quay.

✉ **Ross-shire** ☎ **01854 633230**

### Clootie Dumpling
The clootie dumpling is like a huge cake created by mixing flour, butter, dried fruit, sugar and a few other bits and pieces. The mixture is then wrapped in a dish cloth (clout), the ends tied together, and then boiled until ready. It's absolutely delicious, hot, cold, with cream or custard and in Glasgow and the West Coast it's even fried.

# Edinburgh & the Borders

## Prices
Approximate prices per room per night regardless of occupancy

£ = under £40
££ = £40–80
£££ = over £80

## Room Rates
Hotels and guest-houses will have a board displaying room prices, usually double and single referring to the number of people sharing a room. Payment is per person so even if you are given a double room you will only be charged the single rate. If you're travelling in a group look out for family rooms which often work out cheaper per person.

## Edinburgh

### Amaryllis (£)
A friendly guest-house in a quiet residential area, yet close to the city centre.
⊠ **21 Upper Gilmore Place**
☎ **0131 229 3293; fax: 0131 229 3293**

### Apex International (£)
Situated in the heart of the Old Town with superb views of the Castle and close to lots of nightlife.
⊠ **31–5 Grassmarket** ☎ **0131 300 3456; fax: 0131 220 5345**

### Balmoral (£££)
Sir Rocco Forte's flagship hotel is an imposing Edwardian building overlooking the east end of Princes Street.
⊠ **1 Princes Street** ☎ **0131 556 2414; fax: 0131 557 3747**

### Bonham (££)
A Victorian town house on the edge of the quaint Dean Village and minutes from Princes Street. Each of the bedrooms features an individual design.
⊠ **35 Drumsheugh Gardens**
☎ **0131 226 6050; fax: 0131 226 6080**

### Caledonian (£££)
This fine example of Victorian high living is the most impressive building on Princes Street. Constructed of Dumfriesshire sandstone this is where you are most likely to meet Sean Connery when he is in town.
⊠ **Princes Street** ☎ **0131 459 9988; fax: 0131 225 6632**

### Channings (££)
Scottish cooking is a speciality at Channings, a stylish transformation of five Edwardian town houses on a cobbled street overlooking gardens.
⊠ **South Learmonth Gardens**
☎ **0131 315 2226; fax: 0131 332 9631**

### The George Inter-Continental (£££)
Georgian elegance complete with Corinthian pillars, a marble floored foyer and two of the best restaurants in Edinburgh, one serving superb French food.
⊠ **19–21 George Street**
☎ **0131 225 1251; fax: 0131 226 5644**

### Greens (£)
This conversion of four Georgian houses in the West End of the New Town is a most comfortable place to stay. The Bistro offers an informal food option to the Garden Restaurant.
⊠ **24 Eglinton Crescent**
☎ **0131 337 1565; fax: 0131 346 2990**

### Hilton National (£££)
Modern, friendly, good-value hotel in the busy West End. Handy for the Haymarket rail station and a few minutes' walk from Princes Street.
⊠ **69 Belford Road** ☎ **0131 332 2545; fax: 0131 332 3805**

### Ibis (£)
Situated in a trendy square just off the Royal Mile with practical modern rooms, self-service breakfast and close to several excellent restaurants.
⊠ **6 Hunter Square** ☎ **0131 240 7000; fax: 0131 240 7007**

### Sheraton Grand (£££)
An imposing modern luxury hotel complete with marble entrance hall, floodlit views of the castle from its Terrace

Restaurant and an excellent reputation for fine Scottish cuisine.

✉ **1 Festival Square** ☎ **0131 229 9131; fax: 0131 228 4510**

### The Town House (£)
An elegant former manse just 10 minutes from Princes Street, combining comfortable accommodation with friendly service and an awesome breakfast.

✉ **65 Gilmore Place** ☎ **0131 229 1985**

## The Borders

### Biggar
**Shieldhill (££)**
An 800-year-old castle in 2.5ha of parkland with a 12th-century oak-panelled lounge, four-posters in all bedrooms and award-winning Scottish cuisine.

✉ **Quothquan** ☎ **01899 220035; fax: 01899 221092**

### Gullane
**Greywalls (£££)**
Designed in 1901 by Sir Edwin Lutyens, Architect of New Delhi, it is the only remaining Lutyen's house in Scotland. The garden was created by Gertrude Jekyll, and next door is the championship golf course of Muirfield.

✉ **Muirfield** ☎ **01620 842144; fax: 01620 842241**

### Jedburgh
**Bridge House (£)**
A former toll house and listed building of historical interest standing next to Jed Water in one of the most historical towns in Scotland.

✉ **5 Bridge Street** ☎ **01835 863405**

### Kenmore Bank Hotel (£)
Family-run guest-house with grand views of the Jed Water and the towering bulk of Jedburgh Abbey.

✉ **Oxnam Road** ☎ **01835 862369**

### Kelso
**Cross Keys (££)**
One of the prominent features on Kelso's cobbled square, this Georgian reconstruction of an old coaching inn is a superb base for touring.

✉ **36–7 The Square** ☎ **01573 223303; fax: 01573 225792**

## Melrose
**Burts (££)**
This early 18th-century building is the place to experience the best of 'Scotland's Natural Larder', not to mention an interesting selection of malt whiskies.

✉ **Market Square** ☎ **01896 822285; fax: 01896 822870**

### George and Abbotsford Hotel (££)
An 18th-century former coaching inn with a good selection of bar meals, situated in an exceedingly pretty Borders town near Sir Walter Scott's Abbotsford.

✉ **High Street** ☎ **01896 823363; fax: 01896 822308**

## Peebles
**Peebles Hotel Hydro (£££)**
An absolute gem of a hotel with fine food, a beautiful view and lots of activities.

✉ **On the A702 just outside town** ☎ **01721 720602; fax: 01721 722999**

### Whitestone House (£)
A former manse which is friendly, warm, reasonably priced and with decent-sized comfortable rooms.

✉ **Innerleithen Road** ☎ **01721 720337**

## St Boswells
**Dryburgh Abbey Hotel (££)**
This Baronial mansion is situated on the banks of the Tweed across from Dryburgh Abbey, with its own swimming-pool and an extensive wine list.

✉ **Off the B6356** ☎ **01835 822261; fax: 01835 823945**

**Bed and Breakfast**
This type of accommodation can range from properties with all the facilities of a small hotel to the spare room in a crofter's house. You can find them in directories of accommodation or through the local Tourist Information Centre. But the fun way is to drive or walk around until you see a vacancy sign outside a house you like the look of and knock on the door.

# Glasgow &
# the Southwest

## Breakfast

The great Scottish breakfast is usually included in the price of overnight accommodation in less expensive establishments, but not always, so it's wise to check when booking. In middle- to top-range hotels, breakfast will be extra and can be expensive. A good idea is to skip breakfast when staying in such a place and seek out a small local café where, for a fraction of the cost, you will get far better value.

## Glasgow

### Botanic Hotel (£)
Attractive Victorian terrace house in the West End close to the Botanic Gardens, Kelvingrove and the transport museum.
✉ 1 Alfred Terrace ☎ 0141 339 6955; fax: 0141 337 1812

### Copthorne (£££)
Situated in the heart of the city close to all major attractions, excellent restaurants and the vibrant Glasgow nightlife.
✉ 40 George Square ☎ 0141 332 6711; fax: 0141 332 4264

### Devonshire Hotel (£££)
Victorian elegance in a secluded tree-lined terrace, yet minutes from many major attractions. First-class restaurant.
✉ 5 Devonshire Gardens ☎ 0141 339 7878; fax: 0141 339 3980

### Ewington Hotel (££)
A south-side town house serving international cuisine. Close to the Burrell Collection, it's only six minutes by train to the city centre.
✉ Balmoral Terrace, 132 Queens Drive ☎ 0141 423 1152; fax: 0141 422 2030

### Glasgow Hilton (£££)
This is where it's at in Glasgow. Minski's Deli is modelled on the New York original and Raffles Bar looks like the one in Singapore. Great views and service.
✉ 1 William Street ☎ 0141 204 5555; fax: 0141 204 5004

### Greek Thomson Hotel (££)
Near Charing Cross and Sauchiehall Street, serving a particularly good Scottish breakfast with portions large enough to ensure you won't need lunch.
✉ 140 Elderslie Street ☎ 0141 332 6556

### Jury's (££)
Popular West End leisure hotel used to catering to visitors to the city. Ideal for the Botanic Gardens, Kelvingrove and the Museum of Transport.
✉ Great Western Road ☎ 0141 334 8161; fax: 0141 334 3846

### One Devonshire Gardens (£££)
If you are looking for something elegant and sophisticated yet different, with legendary French and Scottish cuisine, stay here.
✉ 1 Devonshire Gardens ☎ 0141 339 2001; fax: 0141 337 1663

### The Thistle (£££)
Superb hotel favoured by the Prime Minister, Tony Blair, just behind Sauchiehall Street, close to the School of Art, the Willow Tea Room and the Royal Concert Hall.
✉ 36 Cambridge Street ☎ 0141 332 3311; fax: 0141 332 4050

## The Southwest

## Auchencairn

### Balcary Bay (££)
A 17th-century country house hotel on a picturesque bay. Scottish cuisine is based on local produce.
✉ Near Castle Douglas ☎ 01556 640217; fax: 01556 640272

## Ayr

### Fairfield House (££)
There are fine views over the Firth of Clyde to Arran from

this Victorian mansion which is close to the town centre and within easy travelling of the Robert Burns National Heritage Park.

✉ 12 Fairfield Road ☎ 01292 267461; fax: 01292 261456

## Beattock
### Auchen Castle (££)
A 19th-century mansion in a garden and woodland setting. Private trout loch and award-winning restaurant.

✉ South of Moffat off the A74 ☎ 01683 300407; fax: 01683 300667

## Castle Douglas
### Douglas Arms (£)
Situated in the centre of this market town this former coaching inn is a great favourite with local people for the friendliness of its staff.

✉ King Street ☎ 01556 502231; fax: 01556 504000

### Urr Valley Country House (£)
Country-house hotel on the outskirts of town. The wood-panelled lounge has fishing trophies and roaring log fires.

✉ Ernespie Road ☎ 01556 502188; fax: 01556 504055

## Kirkcudbright
### Royal (£)
Comfortable, reasonably priced hotel in the centre of this artists' colony. Very good base for exploring the Solway coast.

✉ St Cuthbert Street ☎ 01557 331213; fax: 01557 331513

### Selkirk Arms (££)
Lord Peter Wimsey, Dorothy L Sayer's fictional detective, lodged in this fine 18th-century hotel in the novel The Five Red Herrings. Robert Burns wrote his famous Selkirk Grace while staying here.

✉ Old High Street ☎ 01557 330402; fax: 01557 331639

## Moffat
### The Star (£)
This wonderful little hotel appears in the Guinness Book of Records as the narrowest hotel in the world.

✉ 44 High Street ☎ 01683 220156; fax: 01683 221524

## Newton Stewart
### Kirroughtree House (££)
A 17th-century mansion in a Galloway countryside setting, the Kirroughtree is a superb time capsule of a more gracious and elegant age.

✉ Minnigaff ☎ 01671 402141; fax: 01671 402425

## Portpatrick
### Fernhill (££)
Dramatically perched on a hill overlooking the picturesque harbour and village of Portpatrick, Fernhill is situated at the start of the Southern Upland Way.

✉ Heugh Road ☎ 01776 810220; fax: 01776 810596

## Stranraer
### North West Castle (££)
The former home of 19th-century Arctic explorer Sir John Ross has its own swimming-pool and ice-rink.

✉ On the Seafront ☎ 01776 704413; fax: 01776 702646

## Thornhill
### Trigony House (££)
Former Edwardian hunting lodge set in secluded gardens and famed locally for its ambience and cuisine.

✉ Closeburn (1.5km/1 mile south off the A76) ☎ 01848 331211; fax: 01848 331303

## Turnberry
### Turnberry Hotel, Golf Courses and Spa (£££)
This world-famous hotel has the grandest outlook in Scotland. Its Ailsa golf course is probably the finest in the world.

✉ On the A719 ☎ 01655 331000; fax: 01655 331706

**Credit Cards**
Most of the well-known credit and debit cards are generally accepted by Scottish hotels and guest houses. Bed and breakfasts are a different story and although practice is changing there are still proprietors who want and expect to be paid in cash. Some will happily take traveller's cheques, but it is wise to ascertain the method of payment in advance. The same applies in restaurants.

# Central Scotland

## Hostels

A cheaper alternative accommodation for people on a tight budget is the network of Youth and Backpackers Hostels. They provide simple lodgings (usually in dormitories), cooking and washing facilities and the opportunity to meet fellow travellers. The Scottish Youth Hostel Association (☎ 01786 891400) has an extensive network of properties ranging from old schools and croft houses to a splendid Highland castle.

## Arduaine
### Loch Melfort Hotel (££)

Glorious views over Loch Melfort and down the Sound of Jura, combined with award-winning cuisine featuring the best of fresh local produce.

✉ On the A816 midway between Oban and Lochgilphead ☎ 01852 200233; fax: 01852 200214

## Auchterarder
### The Gleneagles Hotel (£££)

Beautiful countryside, outstanding range of activities and first-class cuisine make this one of the world's top hotels.

✉ On the A823 ☎ 01764 662231; fax: 01764 662134

## Crail
### Balcomie Links (£)

Friendly, good-value, family-run hotel near the golf course in Fife's most picturesque coastal village.

✉ Balcomie Road ☎ 01333 450237; fax: 01333 450540

## Crief
### Crieff Hydro (££)

Set in 365ha of Perthshire countryside with a unique combination of leisure facilities and accommodation.

✉ Ferntower Road ☎ 01764 655555; fax: 01764 653087

## Dundee
### Stakis (£££)

Next to Discovery Point, with bedrooms overlooking the Tay: the best place in town.

✉ Earl Grey Place ☎ 01382 229271; fax: 01382 200072

### Swallow (££)

On the outskirts of Dundee, this comfortable hotel is within easy travelling of Perth and central Scotland.

✉ Kingsway West, Invergowrie ☎ 01382 641122; fax: 01382 568340

## Killiecrankie
### Killiecrankie (££)

Nineteenth-century country manse overlooking the River Garry and the historic Pass of Killiecrankie. Close to Blair Castle, Pitlochry and Perth.

✉ West of Killiecrankie on the B8019 ☎ 01796 473220; fax: 01796 472451

## Perth
### Kinfauns Castle (£££)

Distinctive Scottish cuisine prepared by an award-winning team is the hallmark of this superb hotel.

✉ Kinfauns ☎ 01738 620777; fax: 01738 620778

## St Andrews
### The Old Course Hotel (££££)

Situated as close to the 17th hole of the world's most famous golf course as you can get without playing it.

✉ 40 The Scores ☎ 01334 474371; fax: 01334 477668

## Taynuilt
### Taychreggan Hotel (££)

A remote place of tranquillity and natural beauty overlooking Loch Awe. Famous for its collection of malt whiskies.

✉ From the A85 take the B845 at Taynuilt to Kilchrenan and Taychreggan ☎ 01866 833211; fax: 01866 833244

## Tobermory, Isle of Mull
### Western Isles Hotel (££)

Overlooking Tobermory Bay with its coloured houses and one of the best views in the Hebrides.

✉ Above the town ☎ 01688 302012; fax: 01688 302297

# The North

## Aberdeen
### Travel Inn (£)
Cheap and cheerful modern accommodation. If you're on a budget this is a good base for touring the North.

✉ **Murcar, Bridge of Don** ☎ 01224 821217; fax: 01224 706869

## Ballater
### Balgonie House Hotel (££)
Set in 1.5ha of mature gardens, overlooking Ballater golf course in the heart of Royal Deeside, this friendly hotel has an excellent reputation for specialised Scottish cuisine.

✉ **Braemar Place** ☎ 013397 55482; fax: 01339 755482

## Inverness
### Dunain Park (£££)
Georgian country house with award-winning restaurant in 2.5ha of garden and woodlands, close to the town.

✉ **On the A82** ☎ 01463 230512; fax: 01463 224532

## Kirkwall, Orkney
### Ayre Hotel (££)
Relaxed seafront hotel offering the best of local ingredients in its superb restaurant. Also home to the now-legendary Saturday night Ayre Hotel folk sessions, featuring some of Orkney's most talented musicians.

✉ **Ayre Road** ☎ 01856 873001; fax: 01856 876289

## Lerwick, Shetland
### Glen Orchy House (££)
A luxury conversion from an old convent building. The home-cooked dinners are excellent and the breakfasts awesome. This is the best place to stay on the islands.

✉ **20 Knab Road** ☎ 01595 692031; fax: 01595 692031

## Muir of Ord
### The Dower House (££)
Early 18th-century building in secluded gardens. Well placed for Royal Dornoch, Nairn and other golf courses, and as a touring centre for Loch Ness, Glen Affric, Cromarty and the West.

✉ **Highfield** ☎ 01463 870090; fax: 01463 870090

## Onich
### The Lodge on The Loch Hotel (££)
This is one of the most spectacular lochside settings in the Highlands, offering a connoisseur selection of malt whiskies, wild salmon, venison and game and particularly legendary home-baking.

✉ **On A82, 16km (10 miles) south of Fort William** ☎ 01855 821237; fax: 01855 821238

## Stornoway, Isle of Lewis
### Cabarfeidh (££)
Friendly, popular hotel with French cuisine. From here you can explore the Western Isles.

✉ **On the edge of town** ☎ 01851 702604; fax: 01851 705572

## Ullapool
### The Ceilidh Place (£–££)
Warm, friendly, cosy and probably the best place to stay while exploring the Western Highlands. As well as superb Scottish food in the coffee shop or the more formal restaurant, the Ceilidh Place has its own bookshop and budget accommodation in the adjacent clubhouse. This is *the* place to hear folk music in the Highlands.

✉ **West Argyll Street** ☎ 01854 612103; fax: 01854 612886

### Checking Rooms
When inquiring about accommodation in a hotel or bed and breakfast, it is perfectly acceptable to ask to see the room before committing yourself. There are some establishments which look grand on the surface, but when you check in you discover you have the room from Hell. Avoid this by having a quick inspection and if you don't like what you see just say it's not what you're looking for.

# Shopping in Scotland

## The Rag Trade

The Scottish Borders are the centre of the country's textile industry, producing a range of fabrics including wool, cashmere and tweed. Clothing manufactured in the Borders is available throughout Scotland, but because many of the mills and factories have shops where they sell seconds and factory rejects, the best bargains can often be found here. Most shops also sell perfect quality goods at discounted prices.

## Tweeds, Tartans, Lace and Woollies

### Edinburgh
**Judith Glue**
Orcadian designer knitwear incorporating runic designs.
✉ **64 High Street, Edinburgh and in Orkney, opposite St Magnus Cathedral, Kirkwall** ☎ **0131 556 5443**

**Geoffrey (Tailor)**
This is the best source of tartan in all of Edinburgh. Kilts, both for men and women, off-the-peg or made-to-measure, plus a fair selection of ex-hire garments for sale and all the usual accessories at a reasonable price.
✉ **57–9 High Street** ☎ **0131 557 0256**

**John Morrison**
Good selection of tweeds and tartans, including ready-to-wear ladies' and gents' kilts.
✉ **462 Lawnmarket, Royal Mile** ☎ **0131 225 8149**

### Hawick
**Chas N Whillans**
Own-label cashmere and lambswool sweaters. Also sells goods manufactured by Pringle, Lyle & Scott and Barrie, and a range of leisure- and golfwear, including Nick Faldo, Alice Collins and Barbour.
✉ **Teviotdale Mills, Albert Road** ☎ **01450 373128**

**Peter Scott**
Established over a century ago, this local firm specialises in knitwear for men and women, from top-quality wool and cashmere.
✉ **11 Buccleuch Street** ☎ **01450 372311**

### Wrights of Trowmill
Wide range of coats, caps, travel rugs and skirts in wool and tweed.
✉ **Trowmill** ☎ **01450 372555**

### Kilmarnock
**Jaeger**
Famous-name factory shop in the home town of Johnnie Walker whisky. Sells the full range, from men's suits to ladies' blouses.
✉ **15 Munro Place, Bonnyton Industrial Estate** ☎ **01563 265111**

### Newmilns (Ayrshire)
**Moonweave Mill Shop**
Situated in the Irvine Valley, last bastion of UK lace production, this factory shops sells curtains, table covers, bedspreads and blankets.
✉ **Stoneygate Road** ☎ **01560 321216**

## Crafts and Gift Shops

### Crieff
**Crieff Visitors Centre**
Offers a wide selection of ceramics, including mugs, plates and tea and coffee pots.
✉ **Muthill Road** ☎ **01764 654014**

**Stuart Crystal**
Factory shop selling both seconds and perfects. Lead crystal glasses, decanters and giftware. Also some Waterford crystal and Wedgwood.
✉ **Muthill Road** ☎ **01764 654004**

### Dunoon
**Dunoon Ceramics**
Dunoon mugs, available in gift shops throughout

Scotland, make great gifts. Buy them here for great discounts on end-of-line bargains and seconds.

✉ **Hamilton Street** ☎ **01369 704360**

## Moniaive
### The Art Garden
Superb selection of original works by local artists/craftspeople. Unique wooden bowls turned from tree trunks, silver jewellery, hand-crafted and painted ceramics, Sanquhar knitting kits, glassware and even locally produced didgeridoos and terribly wicked hand-made chocolate animals.

✉ **The Cross** ☎ **01848 200466**

## Oban
### Caithness Glass
One of many outlets for Caithness glass, with a good selection of crystal glasses, tableware and some great ideas for gifts.

✉ **Waterfront Centre, Railway Pier** ☎ **01631 563386**

## Pitlochry
### Heathergems
If you've bought the tartan, here's where you get the heather. Jewellery made from dried heather, set in silver and pewter and featuring Celtic designs.

✉ **22 Atholl Road** ☎ **01796 473863**

## St Andrews
### Heritage Golf
Golf clubs, carts and accessories, plus sweaters and waterproofs. Also some 19th-century reproduction clubs. Just the job for a new niblick.

✉ **Argyll Business Park, Largo Road** ☎ **01334 472266**

## Selkirk
### Selkirk Glass
Glass paperweights, ornaments, animals and hand-painted pottery.

✉ **Dunsdale Haugh** ☎ **01750 20954**

## Thornhill (Dumfries & Galloway)
### Drumlanrig
This craft centre has a series of small shops specialising in crafts, including leather and jewellery.

✉ **Drumlanrig Castle** ☎ **01848 330248**

## Ullapool
### Highland Stoneware
Hand-painted pottery and stoneware with an enormous selection of table- and cookware, as well as the more decorative gift items.

✉ **Mill Street** ☎ **01854 612980**

# Antiques and Collectables

## Edinburgh
### Byzantium
Antique-cum-flea market. An eclectic collection of shops in one building, with a café/restaurant on the top floor.

✉ **9 Victoria Street** ☎ **0131 225 1768**

### Carson Clark
A seriously dangerous shop for those addicted to antique prints and maps. Wonderful, hand-painted reproductions, particularly of Old Edinburgh.

✉ **181–3 Canongate** ☎ **0131 556 4710**

### Dead Head Comics
Early *Superman* comics, adventure, science fiction.

✉ **27 Candlemaker Row** ☎ **0131 226 2774**

### The Grassmarket
The Grassmarket is probably the most concentrated area for antiques, collectables, second-hand clothes and books in Edinburgh. Here you will find that rare Scottish book, hand-tailored Norfolk shooting jacket or elegant cocktail dress. Or perhaps you would rather have an ancient claymore, some 1960s ephemera or back copies of long forgotten comics.

**Singer Songwriter**
Adam McNaughton is one of Scotland's best-known songwriters. His 'Jeely Piece Song' which laments the demise of the Glasgow tradition of throwing jam sandwiches from the upper floors of tenement buildings is his most popular work, followed by a humorous adaptation, in Glaswegian, of Shakespeare's *Hamlet*. But he also has a serious side, which is evident from his latest CD (➤ Adam Books).

**Mon Trésor**
One of many city antique shops, with a wide and varied selection.
✉ **35 St Stephen Street**
☎ **0131 220 6877**

## Glasgow
**All Our Yesterdays**
Interesting bric-à-brac and collectables from the not-too-distant past.
✉ **6 Park Road** ☎ **0141 334 7788**

**Forbidden Planet**
The Glasgow mecca for comic collectors.
✉ **168 Buchanan Street**
☎ **0141 331 1215**

**Victorian Village**
Another indoor shopping mall for antique lovers. You'll find everything here from 1950s comic annuals through fine antique prints and paintings to exquisite jewellery.
✉ **57 West Regent Street**
☎ **0141 332 0808**

## Books

### Edinburgh
**Bauermeister**
Stretching along the street from the Central Library, this series of book and record shops is the one to head for. Make for the end nearest the National Museum where you will find their comprehensive selection of Scottish and local books.
✉ **19 George IV Bridge**
☎ **0131 226 5561**

**Broughton Books**
One of the best book shops in Edinburgh. You can spend hours browsing here.
✉ **2a Broughton Place**
☎ **0131 557 8010**

**McNaughtan's Bookshop**
Another dark and inviting place where a casual browse can often unearth a real gem or a bargain.
✉ **3a Haddington Place, Leith Walk** ☎ **0131 556 5897**

### Glasgow
**Adam Books**
As well as a varied selection of second-hand books, the proprietor, Adam McNaughton, has an encyclopaedic knowledge of Scotland's traditions and music (➤ side panel).
✉ **47 Parnie Street** ☎ **0141 552 2665**

**Border Books**
Get lost for hours, even days, in this enormous literary emporium. Every book you ever wanted is here, or can be ordered.
✉ **98 Buchanan Street**
☎ **0141 222 7700**

## Whisky

### Edinburgh
**Royal Mile Whiskies**
If you can resist the mouth-watering window display you don't need to buy whisky. Opposite St Giles Cathedral.
✉ **379 High Street** ☎ **0131 225 3383**

**William Cadenhead**
Tucked away at the bottom of the Royal Mile, this small shop has a great selection of whiskies. You can even buy a whole barrel of the stuff.
✉ **172 Canongate** ☎ **0131 556 5864**

### Dufftown
**The Whisky Shop**
Stock up here from a wide selection of local whiskies, although if you have the time

you could tour all the distilleries instead.

✉ **Main Street** ☎ **01340 821097**

## Wigtown
### Bladnoch Distillery

Most southerly distillery in Scotland, closed for a number of years but hopefully production will soon resume. In the meantime enjoy the tour and rejoice in the knowledge that the owner has captured all remaining stocks of this unique malt and has them for sale in the shop.

✉ **Bladnoch, Wigtown**
☎ **01988 402605**

## Orkney
### Highland Park Distillery

The Orcadian version of 'The Water of Life'.

✉ **Kirkwall** ☎ **01856 874619**

## Food

## Edinburgh
### Charles MacSween & Son

MacSween haggis is available in shops and supermarkets all over Scotland, but this is the source. Try their vegetarian version with nuts and pulses.

✉ **118 Bruntsfield Place**
☎ **0131 229 9141**

### Ian Mellis

A traditional cheesemonger whose shop you will smell before you see. Stocks the most amazing range of Scottish cheeses including Loch Arthur, Dunsyre Blue, Dunlop and Tobermory cheddar. You can smell and sample the stuff before you decide what to buy. Do not miss the best oat-cakes in the world, also available here.

✉ **30 Victoria Street** ☎ **0131 226 6215**

### Valvona and Crolla

Scotland has a sizeable Italian community and this is where they come to shop. Fresh produce is shipped in weekly from Italy. Here you can get everything from haggis to fettucini. The café is one of the hidden delights of the capital.

✉ **19 Elm Row** ☎ **0131 556 6066**

## Glasgow
### Peckhams

Amazing deli stocking a wide range of Scottish produce, and open until late. Just the job for a spot of last-minute shopping before you leave. The Edinburgh branch is at Waverley station.

✉ **Central Station** ☎ **0141 552 2665**

## Aberlour on Spey
### Walkers Shortbread

Famous tartan shortbread, in packets and tins with a picture of Bonnie Prince Charlie on the front, is made here and you can buy it fresh from the factory shop as well as a complete range of oatcakes, cakes and biscuits.

✉ **Aberlour** ☎ **01340 871555**

## Fochabers
### Baxters

This is *the* place to buy Mrs Baxter's celebrated products. There's a full range of soups, jams and preserves, along with great gift ideas in the Cookshop. Try the factory tour before deciding what to buy, then follow up with lunch in the self-service restaurant.

✉ **Baxters Visitor Centre**
☎ **01343 820666**

### Whisky

Investigate the mysteries and traditions of Scotch whisky without going near a single distillery. The Whisky Heritage Centre at the top of Edinburgh's Royal Mile is just the place to learn all about Scotland's national drink. Ride through 300 years of history in a barrel cart, passing life-like figures and taking in the authentic sounds and smells of the distilling process. Then head for the bar and have a wee taste yourself or buy a bottle from the well stocked shop.

# Children's Attractions

## Fun for Children

Scotland is a fascinating place for children. While there are attractions specifically geared to them, many other places will have undoubted apeal. The imaginative child will have a great time exploring old battlefields and ruined castles, while the more studious will be difficult to dislodge from the hundreds of museums. But whatever their tastes, all children will enjoy the leisure centres, swimming-pools, beaches and country parks which can be found throughout Scotland.

## Edinburgh

### Brass Rubbing Centre

A 15th-century college church with Pictish crosses. Instructions and equipment provided.

✉ **Trinity Apse, Chalmers Close, Royal Mile (opposite Museum of Childhood)**
☎ **0131 556 4364**

### Butterfly and Insect World

Exotic rainforest setting for butterflies from around the world, plus some interesting creepy crawlies and a nearby Bird of Prey Centre.

✉ **Dobbies Garden World, Lasswade** ☎ **0131 663 4932**
☎ **0131 550 7800**

### Dynamic Earth

This geological visitors' centre tells the story of our planet using special effects and the lastest in interactive technology. Witness meteor showers, see volcanoes erupting and visit tropical rainforests. There are computer programes and information boards for younger children.

✉ **William Younger Centre, Holyrood** ☎ **0131 550 7800**

### Edinburgh Zoo

One of the top zoos in Britain, set in hillside parkland. It has the world's largest penguin enclosure with a 'Penguin Parade' daily at 2PM.

✉ **Corstorphine Road**
☎ **0131 334 9171**

### Gorgie City Farm

Goats, ducks, pigs and hens, along with a cow and a Shetland pony in a community farm 10 minutes from Princes Street.

✉ **51 Gorgie Road** ☎ **0131 337 4202**

## Museum of Childhood

Superb free facility with toys from yesteryear. Show your children that there was life before playstations.

✉ **42 High Street, Royal Mile**
☎ **0131 529 4142**

## Glasgow

### Glasgow Zoo

The developing, open-plan zoo has birds, mammals and reptiles housed in spacious enclosures and buildings.

✉ **Uddingston (east of Glasgow, signposted off the M74)** ☎ **0141 771 1185**

## Aberdeen

### Codona's Amusement Park

Scotland's largest amusement park, with lots of major rides, kiddie rides, adventure playground, video games and a roller-coaster. Admission fee buys a wristband giving unlimited access. Very good value for money.

✉ **Beach Boulevard**
☎ **01224 595910**

### Beach Leisure Complex

With one of the longest enclosed flumes in the world, this is a must for the family. There is also an exotic leisure pool, three more flumes and a massive ice-rink which offers skating and ice discos.

✉ **Beach Promenade**
☎ **01224 647647**

### Jonah's Journey

Take a trip into the belly of a whale. This fascinating activity-based learning centre is ideal for children and they can discover all sorts of information about life in biblical times. They get to dress up, grind grain, spin and weave, visit the local

well and go into a nomad's tent and an Israelite house.
✉ **118 Rosemount Place**
☎ **01224 648041**

## Aviemore
### Highland Wildlife Park
Drive-through reserve featuring Scottish mammals and birds of the past and present including red deer, bison and Highland cattle. A walk-round area has capercaillie, eagles, wolves and wildcats.
✉ **Off the A9 (B9152), 4.5km (7 miles) south of Aviemore**
☎ **01540 651270**

## Biggar
### Puppet Theatre
A miniature Victorian theatre with seating for a hundred. Performances, including a very entertaining version of the Loch Ness Monster, displays and guided tours backstage.
✉ **On the B7016 east of town**
☎ **01899 220631**

## Dundee
### Shaws Sweet Factory
Old-fashioned sweets are made in this 1940s factory using traditional techniques such as striping and sugar pulling. Demonstrations and explanations from the sweetmaker and a taster, of course.
✉ **Old Keiller Buildings, 34 Mains Loan**
☎ **01382 461435**

## Girvan
### Ailsa Craig
This granite island is 13km (8 miles) off the Ayrshire coast and accessible by boat from Girvan. The source of all the world's curling stones and a bird sanctuary, it is hugely popular with children, not to mention adults.

✉ **Mark McCrindle at Girvan Harbour**
☎ **01465 713219**

## Linlithgow
### Beecraigs Country Park
Woodland walks, a deer farm, a fish farm and a host of activities including archery.
✉ **Take the Preston road and follow signs**
☎ **01506 844516**

## Melrose
### Teddy Melrose
A teddy bear museum featuring some exceedingly famous bears such as Rupert, Paddington and Pooh.
✉ **The Wynd**
☎ **01896 823854**

## Skye
### Serpentarium
There are more reptiles under one roof than you could ever imagine. Snakes, tortoises, frogs and lizards. Kids go crazy over them.
✉ **The Old Mill, Harrapool, Broadford**
☎ **01471 822209**

## Stirling
### Blair Drummond Safari Leisure Park
You can drive through this wild animal reserve, with Chimp Island, performing sea lions and walk-round pet farm.
✉ **Exit 10 of the M9, north of Stirling**
☎ **01786 841456**

## Strathpeffer
### Highland Museum of Childhood
This is what life was like for children in the Highlands in past times, brought to life by the displays. Quizzes for kids, plus a regular programme of events and activities.
✉ **The Old Station**
☎ **01997 421031**

### Scottish Folk Festivals
From Easter to November you will find a folk festival of some sort taking place nearly every weekend. Usually held in small towns and villages, they have an intimate, party atmosphere and children love them not just because there is usually some entertainment aimed at them, but because there are lots of other children and new friends are easily made.

# Discos, Pubs and Nightclubs

## The Glasgow Scene

While you will find nightclubs throughout Scotland, the very best can be found in Glasgow, which has more culture per square metre than most cities in Europe. The nightclub scene proper starts very late, and before that everyone hangs out in the pubs. If you're on a tight budget head for the clubs before 10PM and you might get a discount or free entry. Smart dress is essential, and definitely no sneakers or trainers.

## Edinburgh

### Fingers Piano Bar

A late, late club with blues, pop and rock, nightly till 3AM.
✉ **Frederick Street, below Chez Jules Restaurant** ☎ **0131 225 3026**

### Honeycomb

Mixture of house and garage music, plus live jazz.
✉ **36 Blair Street** ☎ **0131 220 4331**

### La Belle Angèle

The music changes every night, but check for details of when to find soul, hip hop, Latin, jazz or house.
✉ **11 Hasties Close** ☎ **0131 225 2774**

### Negociants

Live bands in the basement until 1AM in this French-style café-bar which serves great coffee and croissants upstairs.
✉ **45 Lothian Street** ☎ **0131 225 6313**

### Nobles Bar

Victorian pub setting near the newly gentrified dock area. Magnificent horseshoe bar featuring regular live jazz sessions.
✉ **44a Constitution Street, Leith** ☎ **0131 553 3873**

### The Venue

Popular night-spot behind Waverley Station where you can find, on different nights, everything from house, garage and funk to '70s disco.
✉ **15 Calton Road** ☎ **0131 557 3073**

## Glasgow

### The Cathouse

If hard rock is your bag this is *the* club for you.
✉ **15 Union Street** ☎ **0141 248 6606**

### Curlers

Favourite of students from the nearby University, and also a few BBC types. Live music includes jazz and folk midweek, with student bands performing at the weekend.
✉ **Byers Road** ☎ **0141 338 6511**

### The Garage

You'll recognise this one by the vehicle protruding from the wall above the door. University halls of residence are situated close by so this has become a popular student haunt playing disco music from the '70s, '80s and '90s.
✉ **490 Sauchiehall Street** ☎ **0141 332 1120**

### King Tut's Wah Wah Hut

Live music most nights featuring local and national bands and the occasional very big name.
✉ **272 St Vincent Street** ☎ **0141 221 5279**

### The Riverside Club

Proprietor Cy Laurie's famous dance venue, but don't expect disco. This is where the great craze in Scottish ceilidh dancing started, and not the refined version of the Scottish Country Dance Association either. This is a living tradition and it doesn't matter if you don't know the steps or the dances, you'll soon pick them up or make them up. Wonderful fun and great to see hordes of young people queuing to get in.
✉ **Just off Clyde Street** ☎ **0141 248 3144**

## Victoria's

Two discos, a piano bar with a resident cabaret and regular appearances by some of Scotland's top artistes. This sophisticated venue attracts smart people from a wide range of ages. British Nightclub of the Year 1996.

⊠ **98 Sauchiehall Street**
☎ **0141 332 1444**

## Celtic Music

This music is the traditional music from the seven Celtic countries – Scotland, Ireland, Wales, Isle of Man, Cornwall, Brittany and Galicia. Each country has its own unique sound, but overall there is a thread running through the music that identifies it as Celtic. As a living tradition it is constantly changing, and travelling musicians from the various areas, as well as from non-Celtic countries are taking the music, adapting and adding to it, then passing it back. So it's not surprising to hear Galician or Breton tunes played by Scottish musicians in an Edinburgh pub, nor to hear the strains of an Irish lament played in the square of the great cathedral of Santiago de Compostela. When you head to your first session don't try to analyse or even understand it. Just enjoy it.

## Edinburgh
### Sandy Bells Bar

It's actually called the Forrest Hill Bar, but a previous manager was called Sandy Bell and the name stuck. Even the brewers now call it that. Once it was the best place in the entire universe to hear folk music, often played by international names joining in with the locals; now it's a bit quieter but still a great pub with some incredible sessions.

⊠ **Forrest Road** ☎ **0131 225 2751**

### The Tass

Another of Cy Laurie's venues, featuring sessions on Thursday and Saturday nights and Sunday afternoons. Great grub and real ales the rest of the time.

⊠ **Corner of High Street and St Mary's Street** ☎ **0131 556 6338**

### The Royal Oak

Amazing ancient pub with regular sessions. The bar is one of the finest in Edinburgh, compact and cosy with a real fire. This is what pubs used to be like 40 years ago. Check the board outside for what's coming up and when.

⊠ **Infirmary Street** ☎ **0131 557 2976**

## Glasgow
### The Scotia Bar

The favoured hang-out of writers and folkies. Billy Connolly used to drink here, and James Kelman (Booker prizewinner) is a regular. There are folk sessions on Wednesday nights and Saturday afternoons, but its also good for blues, poetry and a great atmosphere.

⊠ **112 Stockwell Street**
☎ **0141 552 8681**

### Victoria Bar

Just round the corner from the Scotia this is another favourite haunt of Glasgow musicians. The weekend is the best time for sessions.

⊠ **57 Bridgegate** ☎ **0141 552 6040**

## Celtic Music Pubs and Clubs

The bars and clubs where informal music sessions take place are by far the best places to hear genuine traditional Celtic music. Musicians and singers combine to produce an atmosphere that will make the hairs stand out on the back of your neck. But the spontaneity that makes a session so special also makes it a difficult beast to capture. Venues and dates change so check first before you venture forth.

# Theatres

**Dr Mavor and Mr Bridie**
Osborn Henry Mavor, who trained and practised as a doctor, wrote plays under the pseudonym of James Bridie. He was instrumental in the founding of Glasgow's Citizen's Theatre and in 1950, the year before he died, founded Scotland's first College of Drama. His legacy includes a host of small touring companies and a thriving contemporary theatre scene.

## Edinburgh
### The Festival Theatre
Formerly the Empire and now refurbished, it is one of the city's top theatres with a greatly varied programme.
✉ **13–29 Nicholson Street**
☎ **0131 529 6000**

### The King's
Magnificently refurbished, with a constantly changing popular programme and great pantos.
✉ **2 Leven Street, Tollcross**
☎ **0131 220 4349**

### The Traverse
Small theatre with an international reputation for encouraging new drama.
✉ **10 Cambridge Street**
☎ **0131 228 1404**

## Glasgow
### The Citizens
One of the most influential theatres in Europe, with a magnificent, recently renovated auditorium. If you only have time to visit one theatre while in Scotland, make it this one.
✉ **119 Gorbals Street**
☎ **0141 429 0022**

### Royal Concert Hall
Locals call it Lally's Palais, after the former Lord Provost Pat Lally. Hugely successful, with one of the most widely ranging programmes of concerts in Britain. Covering the entire spectrum from classical to jazz, it is also the venue, each January, for the innovative Celtic Connections Festival.
✉ **2 Sauchiehall Street**
☎ **0141 353 4137**

### The Tron
Trendy and contemporary. Puts on some great music.
✉ **63 Trongate** ☎ **0141 552 4267**

## Dumfries
### Theatre Royal
Scotland's oldest working theatre. Robert Burns was a regular, as was J M Barrie. Dumfries native John Laurie (Private Fraser in *Dad's Army*) started his acting career here. It is run by the Guild of Players, a polished amateur dramatic society. There are occassional visits from touring companies.
✉ **66–8 Shakespeare Street**
☎ **01387 254209**

## Dundee
### Dundee Repertory Theatre
Lots of locally produced contemporary theatre seasoned by contributions from touring companies.
✉ **Tay Square** ☎ **01382 223530**

## Inverness
### Eden Court Theatre
This is the main venue in the Highlands covering everything from drama to music and dance.
✉ **Bishops Road** ☎ **01463 234234**

## Mull
### Mull Little Theatre
The smallest theatre in Scotland has only 43 seats but that doesn't affect the quality of the performances, and the atmosphere is terrific.
✉ **Dervaig** ☎ **01688 400245**

## Pitlochry
### Pitlochry Festival Theatre
Smashing 500-seater theatre with a great mix of modern and classical plays.
✉ **Port-Na-Craig** ☎ **01796 484626**

# Sport

## Edinburgh

### Midlothian Ski Centre
This municipal facility, with its massive artificial, year-round slope, has equipment hire and inexpensive tuition. Advance booking is advised.
✉ **Hillend, on the A702 Edinburgh–Biggar Road**
☎ **0131 445 4433**

### Leith Waterworld
More a water leisure centre than a pool, this is a great place to amuse kids on those wet days.
✉ **337 Easter Road, Leith**
☎ **0131 555 6000**

### Meadowbank Stadium
*The* place for serious sports people. Athletics stadium, weights room, climbing wall, velodrome, football pitches and squash and badminton courts.
✉ **139 London Road** ☎ **0131 661 5351**

### Pentland Hills Trekking Centre
Thirty minutes' drive from Princes Street will bring you to this country centre where Icelandic ponies transport you to the Pentland Hills.
✉ **Windy Gowl Farm, Carlops**
☎ **01968 661095**

### Royal Commonwealth Pool
On the edge of Holyrood Park, this Olympic-standard pool is the biggest and most accessible in the city.
✉ **21 Dalkeith Road** ☎ **0131 667 7211**

## Glasgow

### Allander Sports Complex
Great family sports centre with pool, badminton, snooker and squash.
✉ **Milngavie Road, Bearsden**
☎ **0141 942 2233**

### Dale's Bicycle Hire

Reasonable rates from one of the few hire shops in the city.
✉ **150 Dobbies Loan** ☎ **0141 332 2705**

### Scotstoun Leisure Centre
Multi-sports complex, including swimming-pool and football pitches.
✉ **Danes Drive** ☎ **0141 959 4000**

### Time Capsule
A short drive from Glasgow city centre, this combined pool and ice-rink, with various other leisure facilities thrown in, is a great hit with families.
✉ **100 Buchanan Street, Coatbridge** ☎ **01236 449572**

## Dumfries

### Ice Bowl
Offers ice-skating, curling and indoor bowls. A municipal facility with low prices.
✉ **King Street** ☎ **01387 251200**

## Inverness

### Aquadome
Flumes and a wave machine make this leisure pool a must for kids on a rainy day. For serious swimmers there's a competition pool and the usual health facilities, including massage and hydrotherapy.
✉ **Bught Park** ☎ **01463 667500**

## Irvine

### Magnum Leisure Centre
Huge centre with leisure pool, indoor ice-rink, squash, badminton, bowls and even a cinema.
✉ **Irvine Harbour** ☎ **01294 278381**

### Cycle Trails in Glasgow
Glasgow is a great place to cycle, with miles of specially created tracks. Using old railway tracks and canal and riverside paths it's now possible to cycle from Glasgow to Edinburgh or Loch Lomond and even down the Clyde Coast. One of the best runs, though, is along the banks of the River Kelvin, starting from the Botanical Gardens.

# What's On When

**January**
*The Ba'* Orkney. Very dangerous game of street football between two teams, the Uppies and the Downies, played through the streets of Kirkwall, seemingly with few rules.
*Celtic Connections* Royal Concert Hall, Glasgow. Three weeks of music and culture.
*Up Helly Aa* Lerwick, Shetland. Annual Viking Fire Festival which takes place on the last Tuesday in January irrespective of weather.
*Robert Burns Night* On the anniversary of the poet's birthday (25 January) people gather for a traditional Burns Supper of haggis, neeps and tatties, a few drams of whisky, poetry and song.

**February**
*Scottish Curling Championship.* Grown men, and women, hurl lumps of rock along ice.

**March**
*Whuppity Stoorie* Lanark. Winter is symbolically banished by children running round the church beating each other with paper weapons.

**April**
*The Scottish Grand National* Ayr Racecourse.
*Edinburgh International Folk Festival.*

**May**
*Girvan Traditional Folk Festival.* A picturesque fishing harbour, intimate concert venues with top performers and unbelievable pub sessions combine to make this *the* best small folk festival in Scotland. Mayday Bank Holiday weekend.

**1 May**
*Beltane Fire Festival.* Pagan goings on at Edinburgh's Calton Hill. Great fun.

**June**
*Riding the Marches* Various Border towns. Traditionally to check the boundaries of the common land.

**July**
*World Flounder Tramping Championships* Palnackie, Dumfriesshire. When the little fish tickle your feet you realise this is not as easy as it sounds (➤ 59).
*Moniaive Gala.* Picturesque Dumfriesshire village at its best. Procession followed by a fair, and in the evening a ceilidh dance.

**August**
*Edinburgh Arts Festival, Fringe and Military Tattoo.*

**September**
*Braemar Highland Games.* Many games during summer, but this is the one to see.

**October**
*The National Mod.* Gaeldom's competition showcase. A different Highland town is chosen as the venue each year.

**30 November**
*St Andrew's Day.*

**31 December**
*Hogmanay.* Seeing the old year out and the new one in. Traditional first-footing, visiting neighbours and friends with a bottle and something to eat, is dying out. Instead, parties are the trend with Edinburgh's Princes Street Gardens the venue for the world's largest.

# Practical Matters

UNI ÆQUUS VIRTUTI

Above: an Edinburgh
mounted policeman
patrols Princes Street
Right: coat of arms on the
entrance gate to Scone Palace

## TIME DIFFERENCES

| GMT 12 noon | Scotland 12 noon | Germany 1PM | USA (NY) 7AM | Netherlands 1PM | Spain 1PM |

## BEFORE YOU GO

### WHAT YOU NEED

- ● Required
- ○ Suggested
- ▲ Not required

| | UK | Germany | USA | Netherlands | Spain |
|---|---|---|---|---|---|
| Passport | ▲ | ● | ● | ● | ● |
| Visa | ▲ | ▲ | ▲ | ▲ | ▲ |
| Onward or Return Ticket | ▲ | ○ | ○ | ○ | ○ |
| Health Inoculations | ▲ | ▲ | ▲ | ▲ | ▲ |
| Health Documentation (► 123, Health) | ▲ | ● | ● | ● | ● |
| Travel Insurance | ○ | ○ | ○ | ○ | ○ |
| Driving Licence (national) | ● | ● | ● | ● | ● |
| Car Insurance Certificate (if own car) | ▲ | ● | ● | ● | ● |
| Car Registration Document (if own car) | ▲ | ● | ● | ● | ● |

### WHEN TO GO

**Scotland**

High season

Low season

| 5°C | 5°C | 8°C | 11°C | 14°C | 16°C | 18°C | 18°C | 15°C | 11°C | 9°C | 7°C |
|---|---|---|---|---|---|---|---|---|---|---|---|
| JAN | FEB | MAR | APR | MAY | JUN | JUL | AUG | SEP | OCT | NOV | DEC |

 Wet       Sun/Showers

### TOURIST OFFICES

**In Scotland**
Scottish Tourist Board
23 Ravelston Terrace,
Edinburgh EH4 3TP
☎ 0131 332 2433
fax: 0131 343 1513
Web site:
www.holiday.scotland.net

**In England**
Scottish Tourist Board
19 Cockspur Street
London SW1 5BL
☎ 0171 930 8661
Fax: 0171 930 1817

**In the USA**
British Tourist Authority
551 Fifth Avenue,
Suite 701,
New York, NY 10176-0799
☎ 1 800 GO 2 Britain

POLICE 999

FIRE 999

AMBULANCE 999

## WHEN YOU ARE THERE

### ARRIVING

Scotland has four main international airports –
Glasgow, Edinburgh, Aberdeen and Prestwick.
Scheduled and charter flights arrive daily at all of
them from Europe, USA and the rest of the UK. There
are direct flights to Glasgow from North America.

| Glasgow Airport Kilometres to city centre | Journey times |
|---|---|
|  **14 kilometres (9 miles)** | N/A |
| | 20 minutes |
| | 15 minutes |

| Edinburgh Airport Kilometres to city centre | Journey times |
|---|---|
|  **26 kilometres (16 miles)** | N/A |
| | 20 minutes |
| | 40 minutes |

### MONEY

The British unit of currency is the pound sterling,
divided into 100p (pence). Its symbol, placed before
the pounds is £. There are coins for 1 and 2p (copper),
5, 10, 20 and 50p (silver), £1 (gold-coloured), £2 (silver
and gold-coloured); and bank notes for 5, 10, 20, 50
and 100 pounds. Scotland, unlike the rest of the UK,
also has £1 banknotes. The pound is often referred to
as a quid i.e. £5 is five quid or a fiver, while £10 would
simply be called a tenner.

### TIME

 Scottish time, like
the rest of the UK,
is on Greenwich
Mean Time. The clocks are
advanced by one hour in the
spring and brought back one
hour in the autumn.
Continental Europe is
always one hour ahead.

### CUSTOMS

 **YES**

**Goods Obtained Duty Free
Outside the EU (Limits)**
Alcohol (over 22% vol): 1L
plus 2L still wine or
Alcohol (not over 22% vol): 2L
and 2L still table wine.
Cigarettes: 200 or Cigars: 50
or Tobacco: 250g
Perfume: 60cc, Toilet Water:
250cc.
Other goods: to the value of
£145
**Goods Obtained Duty and
Tax Paid inside the EU
(Guidance Limits)**
Alcohol (over 22% vol): 10L
Alcohol (not over 22% vol):
20L. Wine (max 60L
sparkling): 90L
Beer: 110L. Cigarettes:800,
Cigars: 200, Cigarillos: 400,
Tobacco:1kg. Perfume and
Toilet Water: unlimited.
**You must be 17 or over to
benefit from the alcohol and
tobacco allowances.**

 **NO**

Drugs, firearms, ammunition,
offensive weapons, obscene
materials, animals.

## CONSULATES AND HIGH COMMISSIONS (EDINBURGH)

| | | | |
|---|---|---|---|
|  |  |  |  |
| **USA** | **Germany** | **Netherlands** | **Spain** |
| 09068 200290 | 0131-337 2323 | 0131-220 3226 | 0131-220 1843 |

## WHEN YOU ARE THERE

### TOURIST OFFICES

**Edinburgh & Lothians**
- 3 Princes Street (above Waverly Station) Edinburgh
  ☎ 0131 473 3800
  Fax: 0131 473 3881
  web site
  www.edinburgh.org

**Greater Glasgow & Clyde Valley**
- 11 George Square Glasgow
  ☎ 0141 204 4400
  Fax: 0141 221 3524

**Aberdeen**
- St Nicholas House Broad Street Aberdeen
  ☎ 01224 632727
  Fax: 01224 620415

**Dundee & Angus**
- 21 Castle Street Dundee
  ☎ 01382 527527
  Fax: 01382 527550

**Dumfries & Galloway**
- 64 Whitesands Dumfries
  ☎ 01387 245550
  Fax: 01387 245551

**Shetland**
- Market Cross Lerwick Shetland
  ☎ 01595 693434
  Fax: 01595 695807

### NATIONAL HOLIDAYS

| J | F | M | A | M | J | J | A | S | O | N | D |
|---|---|---|---|---|---|---|---|---|---|---|---|
| 2 | | (2) | (2) | 2 | | | 1 | | | | 2 |

Scottish public holidays may vary from place to place and their dates from year to year, thus although the capital Edinburgh may be on holiday at certain times, other Scottish towns and cities will not necessarily be having a public holiday. Major holidays are:

| | |
|---|---|
| 1 Jan | New Year's Day |
| 2 Jan | Bank Holiday |
| Mar/Apr | Good Friday/Easter Monday |
| First Mon May | May Day Bank Holiday |
| Last Mon May | Spring Bank Holiday |
| Last Mon Aug | August Bank Holiday |
| 25 Dec | Christmas Day |
| 26 Dec | Boxing Day |

### OPENING HOURS

○ Shops   ● Attractions/museums
● Offices   ● Post offices
● Banks   ● Pharmacies

| 9 AM | 10 AM | 11 AM | 12 PM | 1 PM | 2 PM | 3 PM | 4 PM | 5 PM | 6 PM |
|---|---|---|---|---|---|---|---|---|---|
| 9:30 | 10:30 | 11:30 | 12:30 | 1:30 | 2:30 | 3:30 | 4:30 | 5:30 | |

The above times are general and there are variations. Shops will usually remain open throughout lunch and even on Sundays in the larger towns, cities and holiday resorts. Supermarkets will also be open seven days and close between 7PM and 10PM but several now offer 24-hour opening, mainly in the cities. Markets are generally open 8–4.
In rural areas shops will close for an hour at lunch time, generally 1–2PM, for one afternoon each week and all day Sunday.

**DRIVE ON THE LEFT**

**TOILETS CHARGE**

## PUBLIC TRANSPORT

**Internal Flights**
British Regional Airways (☎ 0345 222111) have scheduled flights linking the main cities and provide a regular service to the islands, including Orkney and Shetland.

**Trains**
Most of Scotland's rail service is operated by Scotrail (☎ 0345 484950 – enquiries; 0345 550033 – bookings). GNER (☎ 0345 225225) and Virgin (☎ 0345 222333) also operate services on the main intercity routes and to the rest of the UK.

**Long Distance Buses**
Scottish Citylink (☎ 0990 505050) covers most of the country as well as linking to the rest of the UK. The buses are mostly modern and comfortable. Several local companies provide linking services to areas not covered by Citylink and in the Highlands, Islands and remote rural areas there are Post Buses run by the Royal Mail (☎ 01463 256273).

**Ferries**
Caledonian MacBrayne (☎ 0990 650000) has an extensive service covering the main island destinations on the West Coast including the Western Islands. For Orkney and Shetland, P&O (☎ 01224 572615) have regular sailings from Aberdeen.

**Urban Transport**
In the main towns and cities the public transport network is fairly extensive. Glasgow has Scotland's only underground and is also well served by urban trains and buses. Elsewhere a plethora of bus companies compete for passengers.

## CAR RENTAL

Most major companies have facilities at airports, major towns and cities. Advance booking can avoid lengthy waits at peak periods. Avis (☎ 0990 900500). Budget (☎ 0800 181181). Connect (☎ 08707 282828). Thrifty (☎ 0990 168238).

## TAXIS

In cities and larger towns the standard black hackney cabs are licensed, have meters and should display a tariff. Minicabs and private hire cars will also be licensed and may be metered. If not, agree a fare before entering the vehicle.

## DRIVING

Speed limit on motorways and dual carriageways **70mph**

Speed limit on all other roads **60mph**

Speed limits on urban roads **30mph**

Seat belts must be worn in front and rear seats at all times

Breath testing: when involved in an accident or stopped by police for any reason. Limit: 30ml on breath/80mlgm in blood.

Fuel (petrol) is expensive and available in two grades: Unleaded and Super Unleaded. Prices vary and it is considerably more expensive in the Highlands and Islands. The least expensive fuel can be found at supermarkets with filling stations. Opening hours are variable with some 24-hour stations on motorways and large urban areas.

SOS telephones are located at regular intervals along motorways. A breakdown service operated by the Automobile Association (☎ 0800 887766) has a 24-hour breakdown service for members and for members of organisations with reciprocal agreements.

CENTIMETRES

INCHES

## PERSONAL SAFETY

Theft from cars is unfortunately common, as is the usual crimes associated with big cities such as bag snatching and pickpockets. Any crime should be reported to the police and a report requested if an insurance claim is contemplated.

- Never leave anything of value in your car.
- Keep passports, tickets and valuables in a hotel safe deposit box.
- Don't keep valuables/ money in a bum bag. This signals tourist and is a magnet for pickpockets.
- Don't walk alone in dimly lit areas at night.

**Police assistance**
☎ **999** from any call box

## ELECTRICITY

The electricity supply is 240 volts. Sockets take square three pin plugs.

 All visitors from other countries will require an adaptor.
American appliances also require a voltage converter.

## TELEPHONES

Public telephones on the street and in bars, hotels and restaurants accept 10, 20, 50p, £1 and £2 coins, while others can only be used with phone cards (available from newsagents and post offices). Costs are considerably less expensive that using the phone in your hotel room.

| International Dialling Codes |  |
| --- | --- |
| From the UK to: |  |
| France: | 00 33 |
| Germany: | 00 49 |
| Spain: | 00 34 |
| USA: | 00 1 |
| Netherlands: | 00 31 |

## POST

Each town and most large villages have at least one post office. Opening hours are 9–5:30 Mon–Fri and 9–12:30 Sat, closed Sun. Small offices close for lunch from 1–2PM. Stamps are also sold by some newsagents and shops selling postcards.

## TIPS/GRATUITIES

| Yes ✓   No ✗ |  |  |
| --- | --- | --- |
| Restaurants (if service not included) | ✓ | 10% |
| Cafés/bars (only for meals) | ✓ | 10% |
| Taxis | ✓ | 10% |
| Porters | ✓ | £1/bag |
| Chambermaids | ✓ | £2 |
| Hairdressers | ✓ | £1–2 |
| Cloakroom attendants | ✓ | £1 |
| Toilets | ✗ |  |
| Theatre/cinema usherettes | ✗ |  |
|  |  |  |

PHOTOGRAPHY
**What to photograph**: picturesque villages, stunning coastline, magnificent castles perched on rocks and the spectacular scenery of the Highlands and islands.
**Restrictions**: anywhere that photography is not allowed will be clearly noted with warning signs.
**Buying film**: all popular brands, types of film and camera batteries are readily available and reasonably priced.

## HEALTH

**Insurance**
Nationals of the EU and certain other countries receive free emergency medical treatment in the UK with the relevant documentation, although private medical insurance is still advised and is essential for all other visitors.

**Dental Services**
Dental treatment is very limited under the National Health Service scheme and even EU nationals will probably have to pay. However, private medical insurance will cover you.

**Sun Advice**
Strange as it seems in a country with a reputation for so much rain it is possible to get sunburn and sunstroke, particularly during the summer months. Avoid prolonged exposure and use sunblock or cover up.

**Drugs**
Prescription, non-prescription drugs and medicines are available from chemist shops. Non-prescription drugs and medicines are also widely available in supermarkets.

**Safe Water**
Tap water is generally safe to drink, particularly in rural areas and the Highlands.

## CONCESSIONS

**Students/Youths**
Students will generally get a reduction in the entrance fees to museums and galleries on production of the International Student Identity Card (ISIC) or in some places their student matriculation card, provided it has a photo. The Young Person's Railcard gives a 33 per cent discount off all rail fares in the UK and the National Express Discount Card gives 30 per cent off coach fares.

**Senior Citizens**
Over 65s (men) and 60s (women) get a range of reductions in admissions to museums and galleries on proof of age. The Senior's Railcard provides a discount similar to the Young Person's and the National Express card is also available.

## CLOTHING SIZES

| USA | UK | Europe | |
|---|---|---|---|
| 36 | 36 | 46 | |
| 38 | 38 | 48 | |
| 40 | 40 | 50 | Suits |
| 42 | 42 | 52 | |
| 44 | 44 | 54 | |
| 46 | 46 | 56 | |
| 8 | 7 | 41 | |
| 8.5 | 7.5 | 42 | |
| 9.5 | 8.5 | 43 | Shoes |
| 10.5 | 9.5 | 44 | |
| 11.5 | 10.5 | 45 | |
| 12 | 11 | 46 | |
| 14.5 | 14.5 | 37 | |
| 15 | 15 | 38 | |
| 15.5 | 15.5 | 39/40 | Shirts |
| 16 | 16 | 41 | |
| 16.5 | 16.5 | 42 | |
| 17 | 17 | 43 | |
| 6 | 8 | 34 | |
| 8 | 10 | 36 | |
| 10 | 12 | 38 | Dresses |
| 12 | 14 | 40 | |
| 14 | 16 | 42 | |
| 16 | 18 | 44 | |
| 6 | 4.5 | 33 | |
| 6.5 | 5 | 38 | |
| 7 | 5.5 | 39 | Shoes |
| 7.5 | 6 | 39 | |
| 8 | 6.5 | 40 | |
| 8.5 | 7 | 41 | |

# WHEN DEPARTING

- Remember to reconfirm your homeward flight the day before departing.
- Check the duty-free limits of the country you are travelling to before departure.

## LANGUAGE

The language of the country is English but even English-speaking people may have some difficulties with the Scots language when specifically Scots words are used. These will vary according to region. In Aberdeen the dialect is known as Doric, in the Lowlands of Scotland it is Lallans, the city of Glasgow has a patter all of its own and in Orkney and Shetland the local dialect has Scandinavian roots. Although you may not wish to use the dialects, knowing the most common dialect words will ease understanding.

### Eating and drinking

| | |
|---|---|
| ashet | a large serving dish |
| bannock | a round flat cake cooked on a girdle |
| brose | a type of porridge made from oats or pease-meal |
| bridie | a spicy meat and onion pasty |
| butterie or rowie | a croissant-like bread roll made with lots of butter |
| caller | fresh |
| tatties | potatoes |
| champit tatties | mashed potatoes |
| tattie scones | flat scone made of potatoes and flour cooked on a gridle |
| tattie bogle | scarecrow |
| clootie dumpling | a rich fruit cake boiled in a cloth to cook it |
| dram | a measure of whisky |
| drouth | thirst |
| drouthy | thirsty |
| gigot or shank | a leg of lamb or pork; gigot would normally be the thick end and shank the thin end |
| haggis | pudding made from offal, blood, oatmeal and spices, boiled in a sheep's stomach |
| messages | shopping, normally for groceries |
| piece | sandwich |
| play piece | playtime snack |
| jeelie piece | jam sandwich |
| piece break | mid-morning break |
| stovies | potatoes cooked with onion and a little meat |
| girdle | gridle or flat iron plate for cooking scones on top of the stove |

### General

| | |
|---|---|
| aye | yes |
| naw | no |
| muckle | big |
| greet | to cry |
| greetin'-faced | a person who is always miserable |
| haiver | to talk rubbish |
| ken | to know |
| kenspeckle | well known |
| ceilidh | party or dance |
| speir | ask or enquire |
| stravaig | to wander abroad; being out on the town |

### People

| | |
|---|---|
| bairn, chiel, wean | child |
| blether | to gossip |
| crabbit | bad-tempered |
| dour | sullen |
| hen, quine (NE), wifie, lassie | girl or woman |
| jimmy, loon (NE) laddie | man or boy |
| nyaff, scunner | an unpleasant person |
| peelie wallie | pale and ill looking |
| shilpit | thin |
| sleekit | sly |
| sonsie | healthy looking |
| thrawn | perverse |

### Geography and buildings

| | |
|---|---|
| brae | hill |
| burn | a stream |
| cairn | a pile of stones used as a marker or memorial |
| furth | outside the area |
| glen | valley |
| kirk | church |
| sooth | south; in Orkney and Shetland refers to the mainland of Scotland |

### Weather

| | |
|---|---|
| braw | good |
| dreich | grey and dull |
| droukit | soaked |
| glaur | mud |
| gloaming | evening |
| simmer dim | mid-summer when it never gets quite dark but the sun just dips below the horizon |
| smirr | just a little rain in the air |
| snell | cold |
| stoating | bouncing; used when describing heavy rain |

## Acknowledgements

The Automobile Association wishes to thank the following photographers, libraries and associations for their assistance in the preparation of this book:

The Rehersal, c1877 by Edgar Degas (1834–1917), Burrell Collection, Glasgow, Scotland/Bridgeman Art Library 17b; Prince Charles Edward Stewart alias 'Bonnie Prince Charlie' (1720–88), 1732, (oil on canvas) by Antonio David (1702–66), Scottish National Portrait Gallery, Scotland/Bridgeman Art Library 37b; MARY EVANS PICTURE LIBRARY 10, 11a, 14b; McMANUS GALLERIES 64b; MRI BANKERS' GUIDE TO FOREIGN CURRENCY 119; Parliament Copyright. The Scottish Parliament Corporate Body 1999, 11c; SPECTRUM COLOUR LIBRARY 9c, 18b, 86b; HUGH TAYLOR 23b, 24b, 26b, 32, 50b, 85. The remaining photographs are from the Association's own library (AA PHOTO LIBRARY) and with contributions from: AA PHOTO LIBRARY 28, 29, 30, 34, 35, 36, 37a, 42a, 43a, 43b, 59b, 71b, 82b; M Adelman 52b, M Alexander 9b, 87b; Adrian Baker 1, 2, 77b; Jeff Beazley 27a, 40, 53b, 57b; Jamie Blandford 13a, 58b, 66; P & G Bowater 72b; Jim Carnie 6c, 7b, 27b, 67b, 70b, 117b; Steve Day F/Cover (b), F/Cover (d), 6b, 8b, 13b, 38, 39, 64, 64a, 65a, 65b, 68a, 71a, 72a, 73a, 91b; Eric Ellington F/Cover (a), 60b, 75b, 76b, 84b, 90b, 122a; Richard Elliot 15b, 68b, 89b; Derek Forss 42b; Stephen Gibson F/Cover (c), 15a, 16a, 17a, 18a, 19a, 20a, 21a, 22a, 22b, 23a, 24a, 25a, 25b, 26a, 44, 45, 46, 47, 48a, 48b, 49, 50a, 51a, 52a, 53a, 54, 55, 57a, 58a, 59a, 60a, 61a; Jim Henderson Back Cover, 5a, 6a, 7a, 8a, 9a, 11b, 12a, 14a, 20/21, 61b, 81, 88; Cameron Lees 5b; Rich Newton 51b; Ken Paterson 12b, 31b, 33b, 63b, 69b, 74a, 75a, 76a, 77a, 78, 79, 82a, 84a, 86a, 87a, 89a, 90a, 91a, 92, 93, 94, 95, 96, 97, 98, 99, 100, 101, 102, 103, 104, 105, 106, 107, 108, 109, 110, 111, 112, 113, 114, 115, 116, 117a, 122b, 122c; Peter Sharp 16b, 41b, 56b, 80; Michael Taylor 19b, 83; Ronnie Weir 21b 73b

## Author's Acknowledgements

Hugh Taylor and Moira McCrossan would like to thank Mike Blair, Calmac; John Yellowlees, Scotrail; Andy Naylor, GNER; Alan McLean, Virgin; Graham Birse, Scottish Tourist Board and Maurice Mullay, Shetland Tourist Board for their help.

Page layout: Jo Tapper